THE NETWORK MARKETING REVOLUTION

A Practical Framework for Fixing the Problems Nobody Talks About. Learn to Earn Ethically & Professionally Online with Pride, Enjoyment & Ease.

#NWMREVOLUTION

SAMANTHA AYRIS

authors
AND CO.

ISBN13 Paperback: 9798378538171

CONTENTS

DEDICATION

In loving memory of my Dad, Donald Ayris 1946 - 2018

Dad, I hope you're looking down and realising what an inspiration you've been to me, for actually, I didn't realise how alike we were until you'd gone. Turns out I don't much like rules or being told what to do either. 'Two Peas in a Pod' as Mum would say, a pod where we made up our own rules on how life should be lived... doing what we want, however we damn well, please.

Mum, for all the years you created magic out of thin air and made sure we felt loved and the most special little people in the world. (We're still little!) You made it look easy and only now do I realise that it probably wasn't and that mums like you are rare. How lucky we are.

Kev, for being there through it all, the tears, the tantrums and the tough times. Oh, and for nodding and turning a blind eye to my hair-brain ideas when I know you probably don't always agree. You always trust and believe in me 100% and I will always be grateful for that. You keep my feet firmly on the ground and make life, laughs and loving you easy.

It's because I've had people in my life like the three of you that I have the courage and confidence to go out there and help make life that bit easier for others.

Thank you, from me, and from them too. x

FOREWORD

by Nate Wells - Entrepreneur and Online Network Marketing Professional

"The Network Marketing Revolution" is not only a brilliantly written and highly entertaining book, but it's an absolute game changer for everyone and anyone involved in today's network marketing industry.

Whether you're at the top, moderately successful, uninspired, struggling to get your business started, looking for a new opportunity or simply curious to see what it's all about, the knowledge, experience and insights held within this book finally cast a much needed light on an industry otherwise tarnished with an all-too-often murky reputation.

Until I was 40 I had worked a multitude of jobs and owned seven businesses, none of which ever managed to give me the lifestyle I sought. I either had money but no free time to enjoy it or plenty of free time but no money. Discovering the world of Network Marketing was the golden key that unlocked my full potential, finally giving me not only financial freedom, but most importantly the time freedom on top to enjoy it with. The cherry on the cake was linking Network Marketing with digital marketing which now gives me full location freedom to work, earn and enjoy my life from literally anywhere I please.

Network marketing when done right can transform the lives of not only individuals but entire families and even generations. Unfortunately, due to often overpriced and overhyped products, compulsory purchases, demanding upline and predatory recruitment practices, many people have found themselves without the right products, tools or support to successfully grow their businesses hence the endless list of failures, bad press and warning stories we've all heard about.

Follow Sam as she leads you one page at a time along her pursuit into Network Marketing as she shares her stories, methods, tips and secrets towards her success that she's picked up over the past 5 years. Sam's journey highlights the joys as well as the pitfalls as she discovers the huge rewards of Network Marketing when done properly.

Gone are the days of making hundreds of calls to your contact list, being avoided by friends and family and faking it til you make it. Sam's framework means that with a little effort, you too can operate your business efficiently, ethically and of course successfully. From now on you'll only ever need to speak with people who already want and need whatever it is that you're selling. Finally it's time to ignore your upline and their outdated methods and let Sam be the mentor you always wanted.

I've had the privilege of following Sam along her journey into Network Marketing over the past 5 years. To watch a five foot one introvert from northern England transforming herself into a boss, a business leader and now a public speaker has been a huge personal pleasure.

Thanks to this book it's now your turn to follow Sam's journey, learn and apply her methods and build and grow your own successful Network Marketing empire.

PREFACE

Revolution (Definition)

a) fundamental change in the way of thinking about or visualising something : a change of paradigm

b) activity or movement designed to effect fundamental changes

Merriam-Webster Online Dictionary

When I set out to write this book, I didn't for a second expect that everyone would agree with me. But the more people I spoke to on the topic of Revolutionary Change in the Network Marketing Industry, the more I started to believe that a book like this was long overdue.

So here it is.

The opinions in this book are my own and not directly related to any individual or organisation, and the examples given are just that, examples. They do not relate to any particular company or compensation plan. The contents of this book are based purely on my perception of the industry as a whole and on observations and conversations with network marketers from a variety of backgrounds.

But you know what they say… if the shoe fits…

INTRODUCTION

99% of Network Marketers fail.

There, I said it... that wasn't what you were expecting from a book like this, was it?

But it explains a lot, doesn't it? It explains why you're having to work at this much harder than they said you'd have to, or why your new team members are dropping off in droves. It explains why you feel like you're wading through treacle desperately clutching at the slightest sniff of a sale facing no after soul-destroying no. It explains why even though you're doing everything your upline told you to do, every month you find yourself starting over and slogging your guts out trying to maintain some, any kind of momentum.

'It must be me!'

You start blaming yourself. I mean, you're far from 'living your best life' and that sandy, faraway paradise remains firmly nothing more than your depressingly antagonistic screensaver. What's more, your friends and family are starting to distance themselves from you and your enthusiasm for a business you were once so excited to start is seriously waning.

So, there you go, they were right, the business model is fundamentally flawed. A scam. A waste of time. The odds were always stacked against you and you may as well give up now!

Well, that's a relief. It wasn't you after all.

Go on, put the book down and head off back to whatever it was that you started this business to escape from.

It's so easily done, isn't it? Quitting? Blaming the industry is so much easier than standing strong, digging deeper and finding out what the 1% are doing that you're not.

So I correct myself.

99% of Network Marketers don't fail.

THEY QUIT! There's a big difference.

The industry itself has stood the test of time, is about as robust as they come and is a proven success time and time again. Highly successful entrepreneurs the world over sing the industry's praises and tell us that if they had to start over, they'd start a Network Marketing business. The business model itself is solid.

So, if you're doing everything you've been taught to do and still not seeing results, either you're not being 100% honest with yourself about your efforts or it's something else. We **know** success is achievable (because the 1% are proving it and flying with it) so the fundamental flaw is more likely to be in the quality of the education you're receiving, and the stuff you're being taught to do.

But that doesn't mean you get off lightly.

I make no bones about it, success takes grit, determination, resilience and a thousand other learnable skills. Not everyone is cut out to be an entrepreneur, but quitter or not, the one thing we can ALL do is learn. Even if it's from our mistakes.

The only people who truly fail in this industry are the ones who stop learning, stop dreaming, let the doubts get the better of them and give up on themselves. And that's not you is it [insert your name here]?

IS IT!?

It takes great courage to even start a business, I applaud you. The fact that you even picked up this book shows me that you have what it takes. But as doubt, cynicism and other people's opinions creep in, it's all too easy for that initial excitement to fade, the courage to slowly diminish and for you to start tiptoeing tentatively behind others rather than take big, bold strides of your own.

It's OK - it's not your fault, duplication was what you were taught to do right? How were you to know that what you were given wasn't worth duplicating?

But you're not going to make the big time by letting these blips hold you back and the doubts eat your brain. If you're going to do this, you're going to have to do it properly. You don't get shit-hot results with lukewarm efforts, I think you already know that.

I'm here for you and I'll teach you everything I know, but there's one thing I simply won't do, and that's listen to you complain about the results you didn't get from the work you didn't do. Implement everything you're about to learn in this book and *then* tell me it's not working; that'll get my attention.

But first, I need you to understand... starting a business, as brave as it was, is only that, the start, and if you've been running your business for some time now, and you still feel like you're flogging a dead horse, stop. Put it behind you, it's what you do from here that counts. If you're going to be part of the 1% you need to decide right now that you'll do whatever it takes, and this book is just the beginning. Decide to go all in right now, stop half arsing it and throw your whole great big juicy old booty in. No half measures. Got it?!

If you want something different, you have to do things differently and sometimes you need someone like me to come along, pull you out of the passenger seat, hand you the keys and ask, "Why are you sitting here being a follower and taking a chance on where you'll end up when you can just get in and drive yourself to wherever the hell you want to go?"

If you're reading this book, I'm guessing you've either found yourself veering off course, at an undesirable destination, or worse, you're still sitting there with the seatbelt on not having moved at all.

Well, here are the keys dear reader. Are you ready to learn how to drive?

Over the course of this book, I'm going to start by asking you to unlearn everything you know in terms of building your business and your team and start again. Yes, you read that right! Give that brain a good wash inside and out.

There are so many sleazy, salesy, time-consuming, downright soul-destroying team-building strategies out there and I don't want you thinking for a second that I'm advocating any of those. I'm not. For me, freedom and enjoyment of life are everything, so the strategies you'll learn here will mean cutting down on the (wo)man hours, attracting leads with ease and learning to find ways to enjoy what you do whilst making money and helping others at the same time. The more you enjoy talking about your business, the more passionate you'll become and the more that will shine through in your marketing and conversations. A happy business owner creates a much healthier and wealthier business owner, and that's what we all want right?

I'm going to help you to identify exactly what's been stopping you from making the breakthrough you've been looking for in your business and give you the tools to break those down and replace them with new updated skills, strategies and techniques; ones that create leverage and reflect the fast-paced digital world we live in, not the archaic face to face style methods that so-called gurus have adapted for you to use online. Honesty and integrity are top of my list in terms of values, so I'll be sniffing out all the smoke and mirrors, weeding out the questionable tactics and teaching you to chat with your leads like humans, rather than chase them like some hungry sales vulture, as some leaders would have you do.

We're also going to dive deep into your long-term goals and what you're hoping to achieve with your business, then check that your offer and the company you've partnered with are aligned with those goals. And before you say it, I'm not talking about the universe or the moon or any of that other smushy stuff people talk about when they use the word 'alignment' these days, or even just *'Do you believe in your product?'* I mean, ***"Is selling £30 mascara to your friends going to get you that 6-bedroom barn conversion and beachfront apartment in the Maldives Natalie?"***

You could implement every single last suggestion in this book, but if your offer is misaligned with your goals, financial or otherwise, they'll remain nothing more than your screensaver and jealous lunchtime chat! It's important to be realistic from the outset, and if you hadn't gathered already, I'm not afraid to call BS every now and then. The sooner you can start recognising your own BS, the quicker you'll get where you want to be.

We'll then take a really good look at your current method of operation, you'll learn to position yourself as an authority in your niche and unlock your full potential with a powerful personal brand that will attract the perfect team like flies 'round dog poop.

Notice that I used the word 'attract'? That's right. The desperate hunt for sales is over and the hustle is dead. I'm going to teach you to get paid just for being you. Not in a sleazy sell your body' kind of way, but in a, 'she sounds like the kinda guy/girl I'd like to work with' kind of way.

It's like dating all over again. First, they'll get to **know** you, then they'll start to **like** you, **and trust** you and before you know it, you're building an empire and taking dream holidays together. All without chasing sales or filling your feed with other people's products and promotions.

This book is all about creating ease and enjoyment in business.

So finally, the bit everyone needs to know about... systems, leverage and automation. All that techy stuff might sound a bit yawn worthy to you right now, but believe me, this is the exciting bit and not a chapter you want to miss. It's also the bit that most people fail to implement, the bit that allows you to step back and earn while you're off enjoying the fruits of your labour! No more sneaking to the toilet on date night to reply to those few messages, or falling asleep with your head on the laptop when you should be putting your kids to bed. I'll show you exactly how I set up my business to work 24/7 without me having to be permanently fixed to my phone. This is where true freedom comes in and your goal of spending more time with your loved ones becomes a reality. You could have a super successful business and be earning more money than you know what to do with, but if you never have the time to enjoy it, you'll never truly be free. Leverage, systems and automation are the answer to your prayers, the magical unicorn that is work/life balance. Ahhhh...

As a complete novice, I made £700 on my very first sale in this industry, without ever having so much as spoken to the customer. I've never made a list of 100 friends and family, nor have I spent hours on end messaging random strangers. My very first customer is still a valued member of my team today, several years later. She found me online, signed up to work with me and still uses the very same (if not more finely tuned and better quality) automated system to attract leads as I did, all those years ago.

Before you start making excuses about how you're terrible with technology and could never do this, listen up. As a full-time primary school teacher and a certified technophobe, I had little time and no previous skills or experience in marketing. I didn't have a clue what I was doing and barely knew my arse from my elbow half the time I was so physically exhausted. But I was a keen learner and desperate to get out of the highly stressful place I'd found myself in. I soaked up every bit of information I could find and in time was earning 50% commissions on sales of up to around £10k per customer, all without so much as a single conversation on some occasions. Sounds too good to be true I know, I thought so too initially, but I cracked the freedom code, escaped the teaching hamster wheel and learned to live and love life again thanks to this amazing industry. Just one or two sales a month and I'd completely replaced my teaching salary, happy days (though it inevitably grew to much more than that once my team had started to grow too)!

Someone once told me that Network Marketing was a numbers game. Sure, getting your business out there in front of as many eyes as possible is important, but I consider it to be very much a **people** game. Did you enjoy being treated as an insignificant number on the payroll in your job? I know I didn't. Running a business online is no different. As soon as you start treating people like numbers or sales (they hear that 'kerching' too you know), things will go south. This is not about you. This is about how you can help yourself by helping others, it means using your social media to show that you understand them and their needs. Serving people and solving problems is your mission. You'll soon see that this is very much a running theme throughout the book because it's a mistake I see people make time and again.

Being a people (not a numbers) person means I've created a highly successful business online, with a solid team of strong determined business owners just like me. I've become an internationally accredited business strategist, a motivational speaker and now, (she says grinning from ear to ear) a (hope to be bestselling) author, spreading my message and washing the face of the Network Marketing industry, one person at a time.

It's unfortunate but true that our industry has a reputation that precedes us, a reputation brought about by the 'Spammy Pammys' and 'Outdated Kates' of the Network Marketing world. It's our duty to re-educate those who, through no fault of their own, have been taught to sniff out and chase sales like ravenous dogs and show them there's a better way. Go ahead and hand them a copy of this book if you like.

Network Marketing has seen exponential growth year on year over the past decade and has made more female millionaires than any other industry. There's no doubt that it has the potential to seriously change lives, **your** life, in a **big** way. Yet so many business owners remain invisible and are afraid to even tell others what they do for fear of ridicule, judgement and negative attitudes.

How is that ever going to be a solid foundation for a thriving business?

(Hint: It's not!)

By the time you've finished this book, you'll be full of confidence, bursting with pride and uncontrollably excited to set the record straight and tell the world what you do. Because you'll no longer be chasing sales or using any of those mind-numbingly soul-destroying sales tactics you were taught. You'll be radiating so much love and passion for your business that they'll be queuing up to learn how they can do and feel the same.

It's **all** about the people.

And the first person to start work on fixing all this, is YOU!

Are you ready?

Part One

THE PROBLEMS NOBODY TALKS ABOUT

and probably the reason you're feeling stuck

"The first step to solving a problem is to recognise that it does exist"

— ZIG ZIGLAR

1

THE BEGINNING

'It isn't where you came from, it's where you're going that counts'

— ELLA FITZGERALD

As I said, this book is about you, your life, your business, and your revolutionary breakthrough, but for context, and just in case you were considering using it as an excuse as to why I can make a success of this business and you can't (Yep, I see you!), I think it's important to fill you in on a little of my backstory.

I'm not one for blowing my own trumpet at all, some call that a weakness or a confidence issue, but not me. Although I strongly believe it's important to want to tell the world about how you use your business to help others, remaining humble and remembering your roots are some of my core values and that's why a little backstory is so important here.

Put in simpler terms and the words of one of my favourite primary school teachers, Miss Ogley, '*Nobody likes a showoff*'. So, before you know it, I promise the spotlight will be 100% back on you, but for now here's a little lesson in 'if I can do it, so can you'.

I don't have some huge sob story, I didn't have a traumatic childhood, nor was I brought up in a hugely successful entrepreneurial family. I didn't have everything handed to me on a platter nor was I born with a silver spoon in my mouth.

That said, now I come to think of it, I was awarded a commemorative silver spoon for being born in the year of the Queen's Silver Jubilee. I don't think I was born with it in my mouth though, you'd have to ask my mum about that. I think it was more of a...

> *"Welcome to the world Samantha, use this ridiculously small spoon to dig yourself out of the ruts and holes you're inevitably going to find yourself in".*

We were just your typical working-class family getting by in rural Lincolnshire, UK. Surrounded by huge country houses and rolling fields, we lived in our happy little bubble.

Admittedly our bubble was a council house, old bangers and second-hand bikes (often sniggered at by the 'rich' kids), but we were the happiest, most loved and cared for kids in that village. Although shiny new bikes and pristine white school socks from M&S (instead of the local market) might have been nice, in hindsight, what we had was way better.

Whilst the parents of our friends wore suits and frowns brought on by their 18-hour days, my mum worked part-time while we were at school and had all the time in the world for us when we got home. My dad wasn't like the other dads either. He didn't go out to work, and had an uncanny ability to make money doing the things he loved doing, from home. These days we'd call that entrepreneurial. I'll never forget getting in the car outside my grandma's and spotting one of those giant 80s, on-the-shoulder video cameras on the back seat. "What's that for?" I asked.

"I'm going to make films," he announced proudly. And he did.

He made a living producing a whole range of corporate and historical films from home for the next twenty or so years, a time when nobody did that kind of thing. It was the perfect profession for him, a paid hobby. I'm pretty sure that Mum went bananas when he got home with the camera though and that she was left with a family of five to feed on the pennies change. But looking back now, I can see why he did it. He never was one for following the rules, I'm not sure 'working from home' was even a thing back then, but that would never have stopped him.

I was my dad's little protégé and spent hours sitting with him in his makeshift 'film studio' at the side of the house. He'd knocked the wall down between the coal bunker and shed and filled it with floor-to-ceiling homemade gadgets. It was tiny, dusty and bloody freezing in there, but it was like our own secret hideout and I loved it.

It's no surprise that I went on to follow in his footsteps. Only, by that I mean, working diligently all hours of the day and still somehow have very little to show for it. Only I'd got it wrong. I was doing it for the good of someone else! Also known as a J.O.B.

I'd fallen into the trap of being a slave to the system and I'd turned into one of those suits with frowns I swore I'd never become. What's worse, I didn't even have the fancy big house to show for it and just like Mum I'd had to become proficient in stretching a fiver three ways. Gas meter, electric meter, fuel or wine? With no real responsibilities at that time, the wine often won, it helped me forget about the other three.

Bored of an events career spanning 10+ years, I found myself in teaching. I figured I would no longer be just a number on the payroll, I'd be making a difference, and I'd feel valued for doing good in the world. How wrong I was.

I learned to love the job (tick), but I was also totally exhausted, permanently suffering with whatever bug I'd picked up that week and snapped at anyone that came near me once I got home because I'd given every ounce of my patience and energy to the kids I taught through the day. My evenings and weekends were filled with endless, life-sucking marking and planning and woe betide anyone even suggest how lucky I was to finish at 3.30pm and have six weeks off in summer. I challenge you to find a teacher that won't gouge your eyes out with a spoon for suggesting such a thing. Teachers are phenomenal humans.

I was totally stuck in a rut, but I'd made my bed and accepted my fate, and I now had no option but to lie in it. Put up and shut up. Funnily enough, it was my dad that instigated my exit from teaching. But not in the way you'd think.

We knew he'd been suffering with his health for a while, but I for one was not prepared for the news that came. "Dad's got Alzheimer's," the voice croaked. Right there at that moment, a sudden realisation dawned. Suddenly, nothing else mattered. My incessant need to work myself to the bone stopped. And right there, life as I knew it changed.

From then, my only concern was being there to help my mum look after Dad. There were already signs of it becoming a struggle and now was my time to step up and pay back the many years of unconditional love and attention they'd given me. "I haven't got time", my automated response to pretty much everything at that point, was no longer acceptable.

The news gave me an almighty kick up the butt. My dad was living on borrowed time, and I was prepared to hand over all of mine. If only there was a way to free up my time but still pay the bills. I started looking for a different job.

Then the light bulb finally lit. *'If I could work this hard for a boss who could replace me in an instant* (*and they did*) *imagine what I could achieve working for myself?'* I thought. Just like Dad had all these years! I'm not quite sure why it was such a revelation, it had been staring me in the face the whole time.

Cheers for the rude awakening Dad, but it could have been a bit less dramatic!

I had no idea what I was looking for, I'd looked into a franchise and a few other little opportunities (that the pandemic would have completely wiped out now I look back) but nothing stood out.

I remember the morning I discovered this industry like it was yesterday. I was lying in bed on a Sunday morning, everyone else was already downstairs and I had a pile of books to mark and planning to be finished which I knew was going to take me into the evening. The weekend was over before I'd even got out of bed. I was scrolling aimlessly through Facebook desperately hoping something would jump out and save me, and it did. I came across an advert that read...

> *'Calling all Teachers, are you stressed out and looking for time and financial freedom?'*

Yes, yes, that's me!

Looking back, it was the cheesiest ad ever and the marketing goes against everything I've ever taught since, but to be fair, it caught my eye instantly.

There was a picture of a female teacher in a suit (she was clearly **not** a teacher, I mean flat shoes and a dull cardigan are more on point, but anyway) and she was sitting in front of a blackboard (what was this, the '80s?) with a pile of books either side of her, a pained expression on her face, pulling her hair out. If this wasn't a sign, I don't know what is.

'Oh. My God. This is me!' I thought. I frantically read through the post which promised me everything I'd been desperately searching for, oblivious to the fact that it was a Network Marketing opportunity. I clicked the link and signed up to watch some dodgy, hour-long webinar that had me hook line and sinker. I scrabbled around for my bank card, paid my £80 and joined up immediately.

Like the world had been lifted off my shoulders I bounced downstairs and announced my newfound route to freedom to all who would listen. My partner was less than impressed by the £80 I'd just spent so frivolously and insisted I was just clutching at straws. He was right, I probably was, but I was desperate at this point and I'd have tried anything.

As I bumbled about trying to explain more, without fully understanding it myself, I dug myself into a deeper and deeper hole. By the end of the conversation, he'd managed to dash every last one of my hopes and dreams and convince me that I'd been scammed out of £80. My heart sank. Not at the money I'd lost, but that I truly believed I'd found an answer to my prayers.

I panicked, contacted the person who signed me up, called them all a bunch of scammers (and a few other choice words) and demanded my money back, which to my surprise I was promptly given. He'd probably decided he'd be best rid of this crazy woman, and I don't blame him. I plodded on back to my stress-filled job and scolded myself for thinking I was capable or worthy of anything more than my mediocre life. Gutted that I couldn't be there for my mum and dad... again.

Weeks went by and for whatever reason, I couldn't seem to get that webinar out of my head. Cleverly, or perhaps by mistake, who knows, I'd been left to ponder the Facebook community I'd been added to and found myself lost in a thousand posts, obsessively stalking all the members and watching countless 'job quitters' and 'top earners' celebrating their successes. Not being one of them made me feel sick. The more I searched for proof that this was nothing more than fakery, the more I was proven wrong. *'This has got to be legit'*, I thought, *'this is way too elaborate not to be true, and if they can do it, I sure as hell can.'*

So, with my tail between my legs, cap in hand or whatever the saying is, I messaged the guy I'd rudely called all the names under the sun for taking my money (which I'd willingly given him by the way) and apologised. I told him I'd like to chat and to my surprise, he agreed.

I'd never had a Zoom call before (this was a few years before lockdown when everyone suddenly discovered video calls) and the very thought terrified me. Little old me, talking online with some big-shot entrepreneur. It was laughable really. I wondered if he would be chatting from his yacht from some far-off exotic destination. When it came to it, I was taken aback a little. This 'big shot entrepreneur' was just a normal guy. He was your average Yorkshireman, a little bit younger than me and happened to live in a little village twenty minutes from where I did.

'Oh! No yacht? No fat cigar and Panama hat?' (I know. Don't ask, I've come a long way!)

I was instantly put at ease. I don't know if it was the fact that he was just a completely normal guy, or that I knew where he lived, could find his house, turn up at his front door and get serious revenge if he tried to rip me off again.

I chuckle to myself as I write this, knowing how ridiculous it all sounds, but what you need to understand is that I'd been beaten down in my job, institutionalised, hung, drawn and quartered. My mind was doing crazy things and the thought of earning without working my ass to the bone was alien to me and sounded way beyond my capability. This was all massively out of my (seriously uncomfortable) comfort zone and I was uber-resistant to it all on both a conscious and subconscious level. I'm well aware that I acted like a complete loon, but for me, it was all part of the process. Like an onion, I had many, many layers to peel back before I was anywhere near open-minded enough to give anything a try.

I tell you this because every day I speak to people just like the old me; defensive, sceptical, and bloody-minded, and those attitudes have been compounded by friends and family that tell us that Network Marketing is a scam, a pyramid scheme or a mug's game. A little piece of me feels sorry for those people, because they don't know any better, but another piece of me smugly chuckles, lets them go and thinks *'they'll be back when they realise'*, just like I was.

Once I'd peeled back enough layers and was ready to make a go of it, I made a start on the hugely negative opinions of those around me. It was tough, and as happens when peeling onions, there were a lot of tears and stamping of feet (mainly mine). But the risk of failing, losing everything and looking like a complete idiot for even trying was far less than the risk of staying in my job forever and never being able to spend quality time with my dad while he still knew who I was. It became crystal clear what I needed to do, and despite being warned against it, right there, my Network Marketing business was born and Samantha Ayris, version 2.0 burst out of the gates.

2

ESCAPING THE SHADY DRUGS RING

It takes a lot of courage to start a business in any industry. It's never usually an easy decision and just as I had, new start-ups have often already been on one hell of a journey to even begin considering starting a business, never mind actually moving their ass and doing the work. It's no mean feat. Going out there and getting another job like everyone else is the easy route. People who dare to step into the realms of earning for themselves are warriors in their own right if you ask me and deserve to be celebrated in all ways.

The biggest celebration in our house each year was undoubtedly Christmas. My mum knew exactly what to do and what to say to keep the magic alive for us kids. She went to town with an elaborate web of stories and anecdotes (that I now know to be a blatant web of lies) that kept us guessing and had us believing wholeheartedly in all things Santa for more years than I care to admit to. Christmas in the Ayris household was beyond special.

But what has this got to do with your business?

Well... amidst the stress of all the present buying, wrapping, parties, party clothes, food prep and who knows what else, every single year without fail, one of us would inevitably push it too far and Mum would put her foot down. "That's it, Christmas is cancelled!" she'd yell. I genuinely believe in that split second she meant it, but we kids would just take a sly glance at each other, snigger and make ourselves scarce before she caught us. We knew as well as she did that she wouldn't go through with it, she loved the magic of Christmas just as much as we did.

Being the youngest, I was always the first to creep downstairs on Christmas morning while everyone else was asleep, to peek into the living room to find it brimming with parcels. My eyes would light up as if I'd opened a treasure chest of gold and my heart would thump like it was about to burst! "He's been!" I'd whisper to myself, silently jumping up and down, hardly able to control my excitement.

Now, just for a minute, I want you to imagine how that might have panned out if Mum had cancelled Christmas, and when five-year-old me, or you, opened the door there was nothing more than the usual old brown 80's sofa and last night's dirty old coffee mugs. Just imagine going from those extreme levels of heartfelt excitement, right down into the depths of cold, bitter disappointment, in moments.

I see this very scenario play itself out in our industry time and time again. Think about when you first started and finally dared to step off the beaten track and try something new. You were sold a dream, and told all about the many people who had achieved great things within the industry. You were excited that this could be you, that everything was going to change and vowed that you'd break out and stop following the work, sleep, repeat sheep. You invested in products and you started dreaming of a life you'd never even dared to think about before.

With your newfound courage, you made a stand to become the cycle breaker for your family. The poverty, the struggle, the work 'til-we die mentality you'd been bred into would all stop right here, with you!

You're excited, giddy as a kid at Christmas, eyes aglow and your heart pounding. *'This is it, I'm going to start a business! I CAN do this, I'm going to tell everyone and they're going to be so proud of me.'* you smile.

So, with a fire in your belly and a twinkle in your eye, that's exactly what you do.

And then in it comes... BAM!

"What? Do you mean a pyramid scheme? Oh, those things never work!"

"Oh, you're not going to be one of 'those' people are you?"

"You'll never make any money doing that"

"Only the people at the top make the money in those things you know"

"Sounds like a cult to me!"

The comments of so-called friends and family hit you like a slap in the face, a jab in the ribs and a boot up the arse all at the same time. If you're lucky you might just get the occasional eye roll, but we all know what that means. "Oh F Off Susan!"

Your dreams are dashed in an instant. You've opened the living room door and Christmas has been cancelled. It's shitty, to say the least.

One of the major motivators for writing this book is to put a stop to this cruel scenario continually playing out with droves of poor, unsuspecting victims looking to improve their lives. All too often I see the childlike excitement and newfound hopes and aspirations of so many new starters being dashed and destroyed by the ill-informed opinions of others. It took so much courage and a bloody long time to get to the point where you dare try something a little bit different, and now you have, everybody and his dog seems to have an opinion about it.

An opinion based on how Aunty Janet's neighbour's cousin's daughter once got caught up in a cult that went under the guise of selling shampoo that makes your hair grow back. Or that weird woman at Number 24 who posts random stuff on her Facebook page about voodoo and vitamins that improve your libido. What the hell this has got to do with you I don't know, but suddenly you've found yourself tarred with the same brush and seriously deflated.

From my experience, other people's comments are rarely based on direct experience of the industry, and even if they are, I question whether that person ever fully committed, learnt the ropes and put their all into it, because they missed the point.

We simply can't ignore the fact that this is a well-established multi-billion dollar industry seeing exponential growth. Someone's buying these products and as far as I can see, none of them had to shave their heads and sacrifice a goat to become part of it.[1]

And you know what irks me the most? Firstly, the fact that I just used the word 'irk'. I swear 'irk' is not a word I've ever uttered in my 40+ years so I take that back (neither is 'uttered' come to think of it but I digress).

So let's try that again. Do you know what pisses me off? (Better!)

Shockingly, there are thousands of women (and men) out there with Network Marketing/Direct Sales businesses who are afraid to even mention what they do in public for fear of ridicule or rejection. It makes me so sad, angry and frustrated when I know from direct experience the success and fulfilment that can be created from it.

When I speak at public events, I always ask the audience where my *'Network Marketers are'*. Usually, a few hands go up. Then interestingly, without fail, as soon as I've stepped off stage, the odd few sneak over to tell me about their business, whispering like they're in some kind of shady drugs ring. They generally thank me for flying the flag for the industry and calling out the injustices and when I ask why they didn't put their hand up (by this time I've assumed by the shady drug dealing behaviour that they hadn't) the answer is always the same. "Well, I don't really tell people about it."

'Oh I bet you're doing a roaring trade there Christine; all those customers who learnt about your business through the power of psychic thought. Maybe you should team up with that woman with the voodoo doll from Number 24, you might get on.'

Now I obviously don't say this, I've learnt to curb my sarcasm more recently because I understand the reasons why you might not want to tell people. Perhaps you've been burnt before by sniggering friends or you're afraid of judgement, online ridicule or the killjoys bursting your bubble. But it's hardly the basis of a flourishing business now is it, not telling anyone you have one!

This book is all about highlighting the root cause of these issues, fixing them and finding ways to help you inject pride back into what you do. There's a lot to be done to wash the face of our industry, and I can't do it alone...

But what we **can** do is change the way **we** do things **NOW**, and find better ways of sharing our businesses that build trust, rapport and positive experiences with authenticity, honesty and integrity at the heart of it.

Because if you ask me, there's just not enough of that, and that's why we get a bad rap.

So let's change that.

Let's put a stop to all that crap.

Let's start a Network Marketing Revolution!

This is the start of the ripple effect.

This, what you're reading right now, is where you'll learn to do things differently that will get people talking positively about you.

This is the start of a shift, a movement and an upturn. The shift that will bring you success and a change in attitudes that will have people turning heads and changing lives without fear of judgement.

Let's flush those hidden business owners right out and give them a reason to feel proud. And if that's you, this is your chance to stop hiding and stop behaving like you're in some shady drugs ring, forever!

REVOLUTIONARY TIP

It's time to prove those naysayers wrong by being bold and not doing or being what they 'say' we are.

Don't be a hungry sales vulture, be honest, authentic and proud. We're here to make a difference to as many lives as possible.

When we come from a place of integrity, they won't have a leg to stand on and their accusations will be unfounded. Right now, you might not quite understand what that looks like, or even what I mean, but by the end of this book you're going to be respected and admired as a frickin' pro, selling with ease, authentic as hell and as slick as flip, smiling and shouting from the rooftops with your two middle fingers in the air... *"Look at me now eh, Susan!"*

As you start using new strategies to create success for yourself and spread the word of your business in more ethical and enjoyable ways, you'll naturally attract team members and they too can share in your success, teach the same winning strategies you used and start yet another wave of positive experience.

Since mastering a more authentic approach to my marketing, those who once rolled their eyes at me are now the ones begging me to show them how they can do it too. Imagine that! I didn't have to go dancing on rooftops to be honest, and you shouldn't either. Success leaves clues you see, and Susan is going to be so intrigued by why you're so damn happy all the time that she'll have her frickin' magnifying glass out.

First, they ask you why you're doing it, then they ask you how they can too.

As we re-educate ourselves and improve our practice, our success as trailblazers of this new and improved version of Network Marketing will go on to have a huge impact on wider society too. By that I mean those who gossip about Sheila at Number 24 and the ones who offer unsolicited advice based on zero personal experience. Yes, we're going to reach them too. Attitudes will begin to shift, more people will see and experience the value of this incredible industry and its reputation will be restored. Hooray!

A big stretch? Maybe, but we've got to start somewhere. A revolution at its core boils down very simply to individual people, their choices and their actions, and led by an individual such as myself, with a vision and a commitment, we have tremendous power to begin, grow and sustain revolutionary change. This book is my plea for you to join me. We live in a struggling society and we owe it to the folk we share our planet with to support them. We have the tools, the skills and the business model to help so many climb out of the psychological and financial rut they've found themselves in and quite frankly, I think it's selfish to keep that treasure to ourselves. Too many people have been prevented from succeeding in opportunities such as ours because of other people's opinions for too long, it's about time we changed that.

I know, I know, this is only Chapter Two and you probably still have a few doubts yourself. It's OK, I see you and I've got you; all you need to do is keep reading.

My promise to you is that the fresh, new perspectives in this book are going to give you a new lease of life. They'll also open doors for the struggling, juggling parent with three jobs, the exhausted employee giving up a piece of themselves for a boss that doesn't appreciate them and the family who just couldn't seem to keep up with the rising cost of living despite working themselves to the bone. We owe it to all of them to teach them how to build a business they can be proud of, one that will dig them out of that hole and breathe a sigh of relief that a life without struggle does exist.

So how do we go about that when so many seem against us? It's easy. We BECOME the change we want to see, so others can follow suit.

It starts with us, the trailblazers, the boots on the ground.

Are you up for it?

I knew I could count on you, let's go!

3

TOUGH LOVE

"Real friends talk shit to your face and say nice things behind your back"

— PAUL WALKER

A friend once said to me, "You're the friend I come to when I need to hear the truth, not what I *want* to hear". That friend is sadly no longer with us, but the statement really stuck with me, and I'm kinda proud of it in a weird sort of way. Because it's true. I've had friends avoid me for months at a time because they'd got back with their boyfriend again for the fourteenth time. They'd avoid me because deep down they knew that I'd point out that he was a d**k and that they needed to stop behaving like a lovesick doormat. (We've all been there!) But despite knowing I was right, they just weren't ready to hear it, so they didn't ask my advice. I see it as my job as a friend to protect you by saying it as I see it. In my eyes, it's the right thing to do, even if it hurts your feelings a little. It just wouldn't be right to smile, nod, lie to you and encourage you to continue in this whole debacle, surely?

The same goes for everything. I'm pretty black and white. If it's not right, fix it. If you don't like it, change it. If it doesn't work, do something different. And if you're not going to, shut up and put up - quit whining about it.

So now you know where we stand (ha!), I ought to warn you that some of the things I say in this chapter might hit a nerve, they might trigger you, and some might utterly piss you off. But some things just need to be said and however you may react, it's still going to put some fire in your belly; and nothing sparks you into positive action like a fiery belly. See it as me trying to protect and support you with a boot up the ass, just as I would a friend with a dodgy boyfriend, she'd be better off without.

But first a little note on triggering situations. I've learnt from years of my own personal development, that when something triggers you it's usually because somewhere deep down you believe there to be an element of truth in it that you'd prefer not to acknowledge. As difficult as it feels at the time, triggers should be recognised as emotional wounds to be healed before we can level up and thrive. It hurts, but it's short-lived. Think of it as having your bits waxed, you want to shout every expletive known to man in the moment, but the silky-smooth result makes it oh-so worth it.

So, try to stay with me here. You have to face and acknowledge the cause of your problems if you want to get over them. Brace yourself because in this chapter I'm going to talk a little about why so many people seem to dislike our industry so much and how you *might* unknowingly be contributing to that a little. Don't worry, I'll be gentle(ish).

For years Network Marketing was all about person-to-person interaction, home parties, door-to-door sales, targeting your friends and family and prospecting literally everyone you came into contact with (aka your network). There was even a term for it, 'the three-foot rule'. The three-foot rule suggests that marketers should consider anyone within three feet of them (literally) to be a potential customer. It was brought about to force people to extensively hunt down and recruit a higher number of marketers into the business. I use the term 'hunt down' because that's how it feels to me, predatory. Like those sleazy guys on nights out who'll go after anything that moves and say things like *'every hole's a goal'*. Yuk! Whether in business or dating, there's nothing attractive about people willing to target anything or anyone. It reeks of desperation and a lack of integrity and values.

The concept of *'everyone's a prospect'* is still heavily promoted today by some companies, but I disagree. Everyone is NOT a prospect; not everyone will be interested in your offer, we're all very different people with very different problems. Our job is to provide solutions to those problems with our offer, but if you don't take the time to discover what their problems are in the first place, how do you know you can help them? Stuffing your products under their noses to find out is a big waste of everyone's time.

Would you rather risk offending the thousand people who pass you in the street with your 'magic pile cream', or the twenty people queuing outside the Monday night 'Haemorrhoids Anonymous' meeting? Admittedly this is a far-fetched example, but you get my point. I've always found the term 'work smarter, not harder' a bit cheesy, but in this case, I think it's justified.

It's got to be said though, I do understand why the three-foot rule might have been recommended way back when. Before we went online, marketers' networks were so much more limited; they didn't have social media or the sophisticated targeting software that we have available to us today and prospecting everyone within three feet was the best chance they had. The downside was that Network Marketers were labelled as fun sponges who talked business at every party and saw everyone as pound/dollar signs. They probably had guests darting in all directions and diving under the buffet table at family gatherings until they'd moved on to the next unsuspecting victim.

Even now, you might find that so much as a mention of the words '*Network Marketing*' in the conversation has people dashing off to the loo or feeling a desperate urge to chat to second removed half cousin Malcolm who they've not seen since primary school. These aggressive (and often dull) sales pitches of the past have left a bad taste in the mouths of many and done some very real and lasting damage to the industry's overall reputation. You'd think that moving online would have solved that problem, but it appears not.

Having said all that, I have the greatest respect for those who made a living in Network Marketing before the internet, they had a much thicker skin than us online marketers. They learned to thrive on wading through knockback after knock-back to finally reach the elusive "yes" they were looking for. I'm not sure I'd be cut out for all that rejection to be honest and doubt I'd be in this business at all. Thankfully these days, highly efficient targeting and automation online mean there is zero need for chasing sales and hounding people at parties. I have HUGE gratitude for that - I much prefer wine and dancing.

As times moved on and technologies quickly advanced, network marketers started to see the internet as the goldmine that it was. Suddenly they were no longer restricted to their immediate network and had millions of people within three feet, right there inside their computers. Ker-chingggg. No longer was it just a case of making a list of one hundred friends and family (though weirdly some companies still get you to do this - talk about teaching outdated practice) or prospecting anyone within three feet; the world was their oyster.

Many of the industry's OGs[1] made their millions by messaging the world through this transition period, and as a result, continue to teach this as a successful method of lead generation to this very day.

It worked a treat for them, so why wouldn't they?

But most were short-sighted in their understanding of this new technology's capabilities and missed something that had the potential to transform the industry forever. The majority were so blinkered to their traditional way of prospecting, chasing sales and customers, that they missed the fact that the internet brought new amazingly effective opportunities to market to very specific groups of people, people who were already looking for what they had on offer, red hot leads that were so interested that they would inevitably approach them if only they'd positioned themselves in the right place as someone who could help. Chasing sales became wholly unnecessary, yet most aggressively pushed on.

In the meantime, the internet had evolved into this amazing shopping experience where people could pop in at their leisure, browse and purchase the same amazing products and opportunities without being pestered. Perfect for an introvert like me. I don't know about you but I'm the first to do a U-turn the second the shop assistant appears from behind a rail with a big fake smile, suggesting what '*she*' thinks would suit me. The same goes for online shopping, I make my decisions based on my own thoughts and research, not on what a person who doesn't even actually know me thinks I should buy. You'd think these old-school marketers would be pleased with the opportunity to take a back seat for a while and revel in the luxury of having customers approach them for a change.

But no, existing prospecting techniques were transferred straight into the online space without modification and network marketers continued to aimlessly target all and sundry with sales pitches just like they had on a face-to-face basis, regardless of their suitability for the product. The times had changed but the strategies hadn't. People had gotten used to browsing and looking at all the many different options in their own sweet time, without being approached or coerced, and they loved it. They'd become overnight armchair experts and had taken full control of their buying decisions as the choice was vast and shopping around had become so easy. So, when suddenly an online stranger popped into their inbox trying to convince them they knew best, that freedom of choice was threatened, and potential customers were turned off. But as relentless as these 'salespeople' were, it was water off a duck's back. They soldiered on through prospect after prospect, because it's what they were taught to do and what they'd always done. To many, 'no' was simply a green light to keep pushing.

In any industry, we simply **have to** upgrade our skills and move with the times if we don't want to be left behind, and that's what seems to have happened here. For obvious reasons, you wouldn't find a surgeon or neuroscientist using the same techniques and technologies they'd used 20-30 years ago, yet still to this day, network marketing companies and leaders are teaching poor unsuspecting new business owners the same techniques used 20-30+ years ago, expecting them to still be as effective as they were for them.

Social Media in all its forms has made it so much easier for network marketers to directly connect with people who have the potential to be the perfect fit for their business; a global platform where strong relationships with potential rockstar team members and lifelong customers can be built. But instead, for whatever reason; greed, impatience, short-sightedness, or lack of updated skills (your guess is as good as mine), many continued to push products onto the masses with no market research and no real targeting strategy, rather than maximise the effectiveness of the platform's data and super intelligent algorithm.

I guess if you throw enough spaghetti at a wall, something is bound to stick. If you ask enough people, someone will eventually say "yes". To be fair, inevitably some do. I mean, even a broken clock is right twice a day. So, under the illusion that this is a successful strategy, we're told to keep going relentlessly, teaching our teams as we go. Droves of new network marketers are taught these old school offline techniques - online and told 'it worked for us, so it'll work for you' and if it doesn't, then *'it must be something* ***you're*** *doing wrong'*, or worse still, '*go away and work on your* ***mindset***'.

But the likelihood is that it's not ***you***, or your ***mindset*** *at all* (*though I'm not denying that a growth mindset will play a huge part in your success*) but the outdated tactics and strategies you've been taught.

Not only has technology changed, but consumers have grown and become more educated too. In the last few years I've noticed a huge change in audience behaviour, it's really not to be underestimated. Modern-day audiences are proficient buyers, they've been around the block, they've researched, bought, been ripped off by the 'get rich quick' crew and learned the hard way the importance of doing their research before buying.

Your audience is probably far more experienced at being a buyer than you are a seller, and these days what they're looking for is for you to serve them, not sell to them because they're nowhere near as trusting as they once were.

They're jaded, sceptical and wiser, they're well aware of their buying power and have a whole lot more choice at their fingertips than ever. In today's noisy marketplace, people have become numb to most forms of marketing; they're immune to cheap offers, gimmicks and ploys, and interrupting their busy day filled with a million other distractions has become more of an annoyance than a pleasant surprise, regardless of what you have on offer. Yet direct messaging everyone and anyone who will listen (or not, as the case may be) is still so common and widespread and those on the other end of it (random people of the internet) have become increasingly irritated by the constant barrage of sales pitches in their inbox. You'll have to do things a whole lot better if you're to win over even a moment of their attention, let alone have them buy from you, or work with you. More on that to come.

I recently collected responses from a mixed audience of over 100 online social media users on how they respond to cold sales messages in their inboxes. A whopping 98% replied to say they either blocked them instantly or just didn't reply. One told me that she always tried to be polite because she'd been in their shoes before (but then eventually declined) and one said she liked to play cat and mouse with them to get her own back for wasting her time with their crap. One lady told me that she liked to give nonsense answers or pose her own questions so the person at the other end had to actually type a reply, rather than just copy and paste a scripted response. Again, she never intended to buy anything, she just wanted to make the point that personalised conversation is so much more polite and productive than a generic pre-written sales patter. I totally agree!

Shockingly, many of the biggest names and companies in the industry still promote this relentless prospecting by cold messaging as an 'effective sales strategy' despite there being so many more effective ways to pinpoint those who are most likely to purchase your offer. Ways that are enjoyable, authentic and aligned with the honest, down-to-earth person you are. There is simply no need to sell your soul or spend every last minute of the day tied to your phone messaging strangers.

I wonder... are the 'gurus' who promote these 'strategies' even still with us here in the trenches doing it? Do you think they still spend their time messaging hundreds of people a day and face rejection after soul-destroying rejection like you? I doubt it.

I've heard big names with huge followings suggest you find and then copy/paste messages to one person per minute, then in the next breath remind you to expect a 1-5% response rate, like that's an acceptable number.

Excuse me but, WTF?! So I have to sit and message 100 people to get between 1 and 5 replies? Meaning between 95 and 99% are going to ignore me? And even then, the 1 to 5% is just a reply, not even necessarily a sale!

How many people do I have to message to make an actual sale, and how much is that going to pay me in commission? Enough for a bottle of wine and a litre of ice cream to help me feel better about myself after all that rejection? No wonder people are quitting and shit-talking us!

I personally see all this as an exhausting, mind-numbing waste of my time and energy. The energy that I'd much rather spend on something I enjoy doing while my business makes sales and earns me an income on automation.

You may well be sitting there and thinking, '*Oh no, I don't do that, I always try to build a bit of rapport beforehand*'. That's right, as our audiences began to wise up, uplines and leaders started to encourage their teams to '*build a relationship first*'. So off they went, droves of inexperienced and impatient novice marketers inadvertently started forced, half-hearted conversations to build rapport and make sales, because that's what they were told to do. Don't tell me you haven't. Call me harsh but those '*Hi, I love your feed, let's connect*' messages are the online equivalent to the overly helpful sales assistants who pop up behind the clothes rail - only it's much harder to put on a forced smile and dart in the other direction when it's in your DMs.

Jokes aside, I do genuinely feel for those who think it's a good idea to start up an inbox conversation with me based on flattery and then attempt to sell me weight loss products (when I've never counted a calorie in my life), and the jewellery marketers who tell me how beautiful I look in earrings (when I don't think I've worn a pair since I was twelve).

I don't know who's out there teaching you to wildly stab in the dark like this, but please, please stop wasting your precious time. Life's too short. However amazing, ground-breaking and life-changing your product or opportunity may be (and even with a hint of interest), people rarely buy from someone who just dropped into their inbox on the off chance and warmed them up with a bit of faux flattery.

I've been doing background research for this book for some

time now, and along the way, I've picked up quite a few new followers from various Network Marketing companies. On my most recent birthday, I had an influx of messages from online strangers, wishing me a happy birthday. How lovely! I thanked them all one by one, and then in it came... a barrage of "buy my shit, buy my shit". It made me chuckle, but also realise how long overdue a book like this is.

You see, I was once taught to message every single person on my friends list on their birthday too, that way when they replied to say thank you, I could reignite (or spark) some conversation and conveniently slide my offer under their nose. Ahaa.. sneaky! Clever! Also totally sleazy, inauthentic and transparent. It didn't take long before they started ghosting and unfriending me. Fair play. Mainly because, given the rate I'd been taught to friend request strangers, I didn't know most of my online 'friends', and I only knew it was their birthday because Facebook™ told me so. It makes me shudder when I think back to the many scammy tactics I've been taught over the years, but I put trust in the people that taught me them because I believed they knew better.

It took time for me to realise that sales '*tactics*' were never going to get me to where I wanted to be and that a well-thought-out marketing **strategy**, based on honesty and integrity was the answer. I truly hope this book will shorten that painful learning curve for you once we get into the nitty-gritty.

REVOLUTIONARY TIP

Don't chit-chat with strangers unless you're genuinely interested in being their friend or are prepared to help the person regardless of whether they buy your stuff.

Otherwise, it'll be seen for what it is, inauthentic and a dishonest attempt at falsely shoe-horning your offer into the conversation. If you want to attract good, authentic, honest folk to your team, be upfront, authentic and honest yourself. It is that simple!

Consumers see through inauthenticity quicker than ever and continuing to do this is contributing to the industry's continued reputation for being full of fluffy, fake sales folk who sell to you at every opportunity.

All these outdated tactics result in a lot of time-consuming leg work, disgruntled strangers and a whole lot of rejection. Once excited business owners then eventually leave the industry deflated and with bad experiences that they want the world to know about, and the industry's reputation is once again exacerbated.

It's OK, it's not your fault. You were just doing what you'd been taught to do. The frustrating truth is that the odds were always against you because you were never taught new, proven, tried and tested strategies that meant true customer relationships and business partnerships could be built. You didn't see the success you'd hoped for as a result, and that meant one less person to shout about how amazing Network Marketing can be when you do it right!

> **"Sometimes the easiest way to solve a problem is to stop participating in the problem."**
>
> —**ALBERT EINSTEIN**

I dare say this chapter might have brought up some realisations, thoughts and feelings that you might not have anticipated, or maybe I'm just confirming what you already know to be true. Whichever it is, we're going to work through these together. I've created a handy little downloadable workbook to support you in processing what you've read and analysing your current method of operation, with a view to uplevelling your approach as we move on through the book. You can download it here at

https://www.nwmrevolution.com/resources

The workbook is designed to help you dismantle your entire approach to your Network Marketing business before putting it all back together again in a way that will support you in earning ethically and with enjoyment and ease. There's a free version or a fancy published version for you to choose from which will become a thought-provoking keepsake of your journey and something you can look back at and remember how far you've come once you've embraced the change.

So off you go, download your thoughts and declutter your mind by working your way through the first activity (Tough Love) and I'll see you back here shortly for Chapter 4.

4

PIMPS, PORNSTARS AND A LESSON IN HONESTY

Hopefully, by now, you're starting to see that there are no rules that say you have to do everything your upline tells you. It's your business and you need to do what feels right for you.

One of the most common pieces of advice I've heard (that I urge you to ignore) is 'fake it 'til you make it' or, if not those specific words, encouraging team members to portray themselves as something they're not in an attempt to attract more sales. I hope to prove to you why this is not only unnecessary but deceitful and potentially damaging.

REVOLUTIONARY TIP

Every time you do or say something that is not 100% genuine, you're being who 'they' say we are, and that's harming our industry. Besides, dishonesty tends to come back and bite you on the bum; and this little story will hopefully help you remember that.

When I was a student, I lived in a huge party pad with eleven bedrooms, four bathrooms, two kitchens and a lovely cleaner called Janet who used to come in on a Monday and clean up after our crazy weekends. Poor Janet. You can only imagine the state she turned up to most weeks. If you're reading this Janet, I'm so sorry!

We were pretty well known in the area for our outrageous fancy-dress parties. They attracted a good crowd, and it was not unusual to wake up in the morning to find someone asleep under the kitchen table or strewn across the hallway. Picture a scene from The Hangover, and you wouldn't be far wrong. On one particular occasion, we'd arranged a 70s-themed 'Pimps and Pornstars' fancy dress party, where the girls arrived in various states of undress and the boys resembled members of The Village People with moustaches, cowboy hats or leather caps. In true student style, I'd created a PVC dress from a black bin bag and some gaffa tape and my friend, a black gaffa tape boob-tube with red fluff around it. (I often wonder whether her nipples were permanently disfigured by the removal process, I must remember to ask)

We changed every lightbulb in the house to a red one and placed blow-up dolls on the front porch windows as per the theme, so everyone knew where to find us. As we partied into the night we spilt out onto the front lawn and into the street. We even had a visit from the local police and of course diligently turned down our music when asked - twice (until they reached the end of the road that was, when we turned it straight back up again)! It's fair to say that the party was pretty phenomenal... and memorable, for more reasons than one.

You see what we didn't know was that our landlady (let's call her Marjorie), a rather well-spoken lady and upstanding member of the community, was a member of the local neighbourhood watch, and the following week our little soiree was on the agenda for discussion. What we also didn't know was that she hadn't been completely honest in declaring that her beautiful eleven-bedroom house was earning her a small fortune as she rented it out to a bunch of students on a room-by-room basis. Turns out she'd told members of the community that ***she*** lived there. Oh to have seen Marjorie's face when she was then forced to admit to the local police and committee members that she'd *'had a few people round for supper'* at the weekend.

We all roared with laughter when we heard this news. Poor Marjorie had no idea that she'd owned up to holding raucous pimps and pornstars all-nighter. Unsurprisingly, it was only a matter of weeks before we were all evicted, and Marjorie's sneaky little gold mine of a house put up for sale. Dishonesty always comes back to bite you on the bum, or in Marjorie's case made her the most popular lady in town, for all the wrong reasons.

When you 'fake it 'til you make it' or are dishonest in any way about your success to your future customers/team members, you're lining yourself up for a fall of epic proportions, just like Marjorie. If someone asks you how many sales you've made so far, or how much money you've earned, just tell the truth. Even if the answer is zero. Because we all start somewhere, and if you're passionate enough about what you've started you can use that passion to ignite the fire in your potential team member too. Tell them what attracted you, why you started, what your goals are and the plan you've made to smash through every one of them. Sell them your belief! It makes you so much more relatable; more relatable than someone like me who's been around a while and is achieving ranks that to a complete beginner feel totally out of reach and unobtainable, so why lie? You're at least one step ahead of them in their journey which means you have what *they* want and therefore are already inspirational in their eyes.

So rather than 'Fake it 'til you make it', try 'Be it until you see it'. BE yourself; a person with integrity, who's genuine and never fakes anything. God knows there's enough of that on the internet. It's refreshing to come across someone who's being real, raw and honest; people appreciate honesty more than anything. Besides, they're going to get to know the real you when they join you anyway and finding out your upline wasn't upfront with you from day dot is hardly the foundations of a solid lifelong business relationship now is it?

REVOLUTIONARY TIP

If you want to sell a rags-to-riches success story, do the work and become one. In the meantime, use the success of those around you as an example; your time will come.

If you've done (or still do) any of the things I've mentioned in the last couple of chapters, don't worry. I did too to some degree before I knew better. It's not your fault. You're just doing what you were taught to do because you trusted that the person teaching you this stuff might have a clue what they're talking about. Maybe it worked for them, three, five, or ten years ago when things were very different; just not today. I'm so pleased to tell you that you don't need to fake a thing and that you don't need to have any of those awkward AF messenger conversations ever again either, because I'm going to teach you a much easier, more enjoyable and more ethical way of earning money online.

One last thing before we go on, I want you to take the time to congratulate yourself. So many before you never made it as far as you have in this business. You're still here despite your struggles and you didn't come this far to only come this far. You've got balls (or boobs) of steel and you're ready to start righting wrongs. You also made it through the toughest chapters of the book where I told you that those things you might have been doing, are most likely the reason you're not where you hoped you'd be by now and exactly why our industry gets a bad name. It's OK. I know you never meant to contribute to that. You don't know what you don't know.

But now you do, 'meaning well' means nothing without action. It takes courage to turn our backs or disagree with the leaders who have brought us this far but remaining silent and continuing to follow the crowd when things are just not working for you doesn't help anyone either. It's much easier to be a follower and keep the peace, but when something doesn't feel right or isn't working for you, it makes no sense to carry on doing it just because everyone else is. That's what got us into this mess in the first place.

Remember...

"If you always do what you always did, you'll always get what you always got"

— HENRY FORD.

This is your business, your life and your future at stake here, no one else's. People are not going to be upset with you for long when you reveal you've found a new, more enjoyable way of earning with ease; they're going to want to know how you did it, the roles will reverse, and **you** will find yourself being the revolutionary leader. Remember what I said, if it's not working, change it, if you're not happy, do something about it. Everyone should feel like they're supported in standing up for what they believe in and even if those around you don't. I do, and so do the many people I've taught these revolutionary new strategies to too. Remember, by calling out outdated practice (especially when you know so many other people silently agree that it's not working but daren't do anything about it), we have the power to set off a ripple effect strong enough to create a movement and positive shift in the entire industry. We're starting a revolution that's going to change the lives of so many more people. We owe it to them. You owe it to yourself.

5

LOOK WITHIN OR GO WITHOUT

"When you blame others, you give up your power to change"

— ROBERT ANTHONY

As Network Marketers, personal development and not having the right 'mindset' is often pushed upon us as a way of making us accept responsibility for a failing business. There is, without a doubt, a correlation between mindset, self-belief and success and I could very easily have written a book about how important it is to have your mind monkeys in a row before starting in business, because it is! But there's also this huge, great elephant in the room that isn't talked about... you can be the most positive person in the world, read every personal development book on the planet and have a Master's degree in the Law of Attraction, but without a proven, tried and tested marketing strategy **that works,** and **consistent and determined action**, your business is going nowhere.

I guess if you've just started and are about to be taught to spend your days glued to your phone cold messaging strangers who never reply, your upline needs you to become one motivated, resilient go-getter, and fast. There's no wonder we were all plunged into the personal development sheep dip on entry. I, like many people, was one of those who said, *'Oh there's nothing wrong with my mindset, just show me how to make money'*, I thought personal development was for people with "*problems*", and all I wanted was to do the practical stuff and start earning in as little time as possible. Months later when the money still wasn't rolling in consistently, despite following all the guidance and training, (and once I'd finished blaming everyone else) I realised that I wasn't acting like a business owner at all. I was impatient, short sighted and expected just to be able to watch a few pieces of training, put a few posts out and watch the money float from the sky. I learnt the hard way that it just doesn't work like that.

That said, no amount of 'working on yourself' can compensate for shoddy, or non existent marketing strategy either, and what I don't like to see is people 'doing the work on themselves' then beating themselves up and blaming themselves for their lack of success when it's clear to me that the strategies (if we can call them that) being taught are not exactly cutting them any slack either.

It would be easy to take everything we've spoken about so far and start the blame game, but it's important to remember at this stage that your upline isn't responsible for your success. You are. Even if you weren't provided with the greatest support or the best training available, it's your responsibility to recognise that and react to it by altering your trajectory. I hope what we've covered so far in this book has helped you recognise where you might be going wrong and start thinking about how you might react. Your reaction is important, it's a choice, and blaming others for something which is essentially your responsibility is never the answer.

We all have a tendency to slip into victim mode from time to time and blame everyone around us when things are not going our way, but there's only one person in control of where your life is headed, and that's you. You are where you are right now because of the choices and decisions you made to get you here, some good, some not so good. So shall we sit here and complain about where we've found ourselves, or shall we put our entrepreneurial heads on to do everything in our power to turn things around? That involves dissecting your part in this too. Part two of this book will support you in reacting positively and changing the trajectory entirely if that's what you feel you need to do, but first I want you to ask yourself this one question. Have you **really** been giving it your all?

Self-awareness is so important. We all need the ability to stop, step back and take a bird's eye view of ourselves sometimes. Without self-awareness we don't have the ability to shift or change, because we don't recognise the need to. Ask yourself, am I pulling out all the stops? Why do I do the things I do? What's stopping me from seeing success in life and business, and why isn't it growing as I'd like it to? What's my part in this?

Recognising and calling yourself out on your own BS is a major breakthrough, as long as you follow it up with the action of course (I see that happen a lot too, you know who you are). It's so easy to blame everything else around us for why we don't have the results we desire, but more often than not we're also our own biggest obstacle. When you don't take the time to step back and evaluate your own actions, you just continue to do the same things over and over, which creates the same result time and time again, and when you continue to do things the same way all the time, you're not evolving or growing. You become stagnant and that leads to frustration because you don't feel like you're getting anywhere. Because you're not!

This is the moment you need to **decide** to take radical self-responsibility for every area of your life from this point on, because in the words of the wonderful Mel Robbins, **'No one is coming to save you'**. No one is coming to push you. It's all up to YOU.

I can give you the tools, a manual and the parts to build your Ferrari, but you're the one who has to use those tools to build it and put the fuel in if you want the Ferrari lifestyle.

I can help you with the Ferrari of a business model, the training and the proven, tried and tested marketing strategy but the rest is down to you. I can't make it happen for you, you need to **discipline yourself** and **act** if you want to make radical changes in your life.

Accepting responsibility when everything is going right is easy, we all do it, but self-reflection isn't about who you are when things are going right, it's how you act when things are not going well, when nothing feels right, when your business isn't going to plan and the money just isn't flowing in. It's how you choose to act in those moments that determine how successful you're going to be.

It's not a time to be pointing fingers and blaming others, it's time to look at yourself and think, *'Damn, that was a bad decision, what shall I do to rectify that and keep me on course?'* It's down to you and you alone to embrace what isn't working and make change happen. That may feel daunting, but when you **decide** to become radically responsible for every area of your life, the good and the bad, and when you're willing to explore and question the way you react to things, why certain things trigger you, why you show up the way you do and why some things go wrong, you'll feel liberated. Because **you** are in control of everything, it's just a matter of making better choices and better decisions. **You** are steering this ship, don't forget that, and **you** have the freedom to sail off into the sunset at any given moment, one decision at a time.

So stop thinking about where you came from, or what's happened. Draw a line under it; it's what you do from here on out that matters. It's time to take back control and do it **your way.**

The Trifecta of Triumph

The 'Trifecta of Triumph' demonstrates the delicate balance required to successfully run your business.

- An irresistible offer and effective marketing strategy/toolkit
- Unshakeable belief
- Consistent and determined action

In my experience, all are equally important and you're unlikely to see true triumph in business until you've mastered all three simultaneously. If you're missing just one element of the Trifecta, you're likely to encounter hurdles. Missing two; struggle is inevitable and missing all three? Well, you're kidding yourself and don't have a business at all, never mind one destined for triumph.

THE TRIFECTA OF TRIUMPH

Consistent & Determined Action + Unshakeable Belief - Irresistible Offer & Effective Strategy = Deflated Marketer

Find an offer that's irresistible to your audience and a proven marketing strategy to attract them in their droves - see Part Two.

Unshakeable Belief + Irresistible Offer & Effective Strategy - Consistent Action = Slow Progress

Crack on and make the time to build solid foundations for your business. You can sit back and rest on your laurels once you're starting to see a consistent income, but not until. (*Use the **#nwmrevolution** workbook to uncover why you're procrastinating on taking consistent action, you'll find some questions there that will help you get to the bottom of it*

www.nwmrevolution.com/resources

Consistent & Determined Action + Irresistible Offer & Effective Strategy - Unshakeable Belief = Eventual Procrastination Hindering Progress

Is it a belief in yourself and your ability to become successful that's holding you back? Or is it the lack of belief that your current offer can get you there that's the problem? (Use the 'Belief' section of your **#nwmrevolution** workbook to help you find a solution. *www.nwmrevolution.com/resources*)

REVOLUTIONARY TASK

Hopefully, you've already started on a bit of this self reflection in your head as you've been reading, and you'll know instinctively whether you've really been giving it your all. There are, of course always reasons for not going all in and taking action, even when deep down you know it will be beneficial, but your **#nwmrevolution** workbook will help you uncover those and give you the space to find a way to move forward. (*www.nwmrevolution.com/resources*)

Whilst this may feel uncomfortable, you will start to enjoy the freedom that this gives you. Self-awareness gives you the ability to step out of being the victim and into your innate capability to create exactly what it is you desire, and that's exciting.

6

THE NOT SO SIMPLE QUESTION...WHAT DO YOU WANT?

"What do you want? What do you want? WHAT DO YOU WANT?"

— RYAN GOSLING - THE NOTEBOOK.

Reading this book, the old me would be thinking, *'Oh, here's the obligatory 'goal setting' chapter! Enough of this waffle; just give me what I need to make money!'*

Fair point, goal setting is covered in just about every book I've ever read, and that's exactly why I'm not going to get you creating a vision board, meditating and visualising your 'dream life' every morning. Yes, there's relevance in all that, I'm not dissing it at all, but my bets are still on needing to take some very real, focused action to make things happen too. My reasons for a goal setting 'style' chapter are very different. We can't create a strategy, if we don't know where we're going.

Let's see, you started out on this entrepreneurial journey for one of two reasons. Either to..

1. Achieve something (positive) or
2. Avoid something (negative)

You're either trying to move away from pain (like I was, trying to get out of my job to make more time) or looking for more pleasure (because, well, there's more to life), but either way, you're looking for an outcome and creating a plan on how best to achieve that outcome is vital if you're going to achieve it. We're not talking lackadaisical dreaming here, this is daring to think big, then working backwards to break down the elements and create a plan on how you're going to achieve it - strategically. Daring to dream about things you feel are out of reach, as whimsical as it sounds, is just an essential start to the process.

Back in the days when I was doing my coaching accreditation, it turned out to be as much about being coached myself as learning to coach others. You've got to learn to walk the walk, not just talk the talk, right? I was still in my full-time teaching job at the time and I was very much on the negative end of the scale. All I wanted was to end the pain, the stress, the long hours, and the lack of work/life balance and I found it difficult to see past all that. My coach relentlessly pushed me to set goals and would constantly ask me 'What do you want [in life]?' My replies were always along the lines of, I just don't want to be in this job anymore, I don't want to feel this way anymore, I'm tired and frustrated and I don't want to be this permanently exhausted shadow of a person who can't even be there for her family when they need me'.

And like Ryan Gosling in that famous scene in The Notebook (if you haven't seen it you need to) he'd come back with, "*OK so now I know what you don't want, what DO you want? What do you want? What do you want? WHAT DO YOU WANT?*"

Feeling a mixture of anger, frustration and confusion, I couldn't answer. Did he want me to make something up? Because I seriously had nothing! I was in such a deep hole that all I could see was the darkness I'd found myself in. I'd stopped dreaming and believing that there was anything else out there for me. I was stuck and literally couldn't even imagine myself being anywhere but the place I was in, and that right there was the problem. If you can't picture a brighter future, how the hell are you going to plan to get there?

It's an overused analogy but, if you're planning to drive from one end of the country to the other, you don't just jump in, start driving and hope for the best. You make a plan, you figure out how you're going to get there or at the very least type the destination into your satnav. Even my Dad, who insisted he was an expert in long journeys, used to briefly cast his eyes over the map before setting off, before we inevitably found ourselves in the middle of nowhere and having to admit we were lost.

I was encouraged by my coach to set the satnav, think big and visualise achieving my wildest dreams. I hated it. All I could focus on was 'but how?' and visualising something that felt unattainable to me felt difficult, painful and pointless because all it did was remind me of what everyone else seemed to have and what I'd failed to achieve so far. My partner would spend hours on end looking at what I deemed to be ridiculously priced cars for sale online. I distinctly remember asking him one night, *'Why do you even bother looking at cars you'll never be able to afford?'*

'Ahh You never know!', he replied as if he'd fixed a lottery win or something. I shook my head and rolled my eyes thinking what a soul-destroying waste of time it was. He's now driving around in one of those 'ridiculously priced cars' and it wasn't from a lottery win either. Lesson learnt.

Imagine being handed a bow and arrow and encouraged to hit a target you can't see. You don't know what it looks like, or even which direction it's in. Even with all the skills, training and most technologically advanced bow and arrow in the world, do you think you're likely to hit it? Of course not. Likewise, unless you have a clear vision and belief of yourself living in that 6 bedroomed barn conversion with stables and a little picket fence, you're unlikely to get there. And unless you believe you have what it takes to build a business to pay for it, you won't.

'Whether you think you can, or think you can't, you're right'

— HENRY FORD.

Just read that again and let it sink in. If you don't believe you can achieve success in your business by doing what you're already doing, it's unlikely to happen. It also means it's probably time you started doing things differently to help fill your belief bucket with evidence and wins that start proving to yourself that you can. Part Two of this book's going to help you do that.

As easy as it is to be drawn in by it, **how** you achieve this is not important right now, what is important is knowing that **'whatever the mind can conceive and believe, it can achieve'** Napoleon Hill (*I'm totally unapologetic about throwing in all these overused quotes by the way, they're overused for a reason - they're 100% accurate and relevant*)

Before we move on to the strategies and practicalities of achieving these goals, you need to get super clear on what you're working towards. **What do you want?** I'm not going to run you through 'how' to set goals, you can find that in a million other books, but I do want you to think big. What would make you truly, truly happy? What does that dream lifestyle look like to you? You can get your copy **of the #nwmrevolution workbook** at www.nwmrevolution.com/resources to record them.

If you're struggling with this, try going back to your core values. What's most important to you?

REVOLUTIONARY TASK

In the **#nwmrevolution** workbook, there's an exercise in sorting your core values in order of importance; you might also call these your priorities. Here's an example of some of the core values for you to prioritise. How you rank these values will help you to uncover whether your current business plan and method of operation are likely to get you there.

- Quality time with friends and family
- Solid work ethic/career
- Financial freedom/wealth
- Health and Wellbeing
- Freedom to travel/work remotely
- Education and Learning
- Looking after the planet
- Networking/Meeting new people
- Working on something you're proud of
- Time Freedom/control of own schedule
- Supporting the community

At the moment, they may feel more wishful thinking than actual goals, but that's ok. Nothing brings you back to earth with a bump like putting a monetary amount to them, which is what we're going to do now. Knowing how much you'll need to make them happen is the transition your brain needs to go from 'dream' to 'goal', 'goal' to 'ACTION', and is the key step most people miss.

So go on, complete this exercise in your **#nwmrevolution** workbook and work out precisely how much are you going to need every single month to actually live this dream lifestyle. Work it out. Do your research. Search online estate agents, travel agents, whatever it is you need to find out how much these things cost. Most tell me it's a strangely exciting experience and somehow, just by committing it to paper, makes it feel like one step closer to reality. Some even say the result turned out to be far more realistic and achievable than they once thought. How about you? Share with us using hashtag **#nwmrevolution**. Use your **#nwmrevolution** workbook to write yourself a monthly budget including everything you'll need to make this a reality. Don't forget to leave yourself some spending money too, the world is your oyster.

Once you've done this (and make sure you do, this is not the step you want to miss) we can start putting plans into place and make sure that your current business strategy is aligned with your vision, and if it's not, we can start thinking about the changes you need to make to match them up. This is all coming up in Part Two.

7

THE WORST TIME TO BUILD A BUSINESS OR THE GREATEST OPPORTUNITY OF YOUR LIFE?

A little, but crucial caveat

'Fortune Favours the Brave'

— **LATIN PROVERB**

I just wanted to jump into a quick caveat here, as at the time of writing this book we're entering a period of recession; the cost of living, interest rates, everything is soaring rapidly, and many people are really starting to feel the pinch. Nobody knows how long this will last or how deep a recession this will become, and it's making people feel uneasy. So, you may well be reading this book and thinking that now's really not the best time to be dreaming up such frivolous and audacious goals and that instead, you should be finding ways to cut costs and live more minimalistically. I understand where you're coming from, but I disagree.

Any true entrepreneur will tell you that times of economic struggle are opportunities of a lifetime. This is the opportunity of **your** lifetime. Now is the time to act, dream, pivot, to make big moves. Why? Because when everyone else retreats into their snail shells, entrepreneurial action-takers advance. Fortune favours the brave (Latin proverb). There have been endless well-known organisations started in times of crisis, Uber, Microsoft, and Disney; go ahead and Google them for yourself, it's another book in itself.

Remember what we spoke about right at the beginning, **it's not how you act when things are going to plan, it's how you act when the shit hits the fan. #nwmrevolution** This is your time to shine and show the world what you're made of. It's imperative to cultivate a positive attitude towards this recession, or whatever other adversities you may be facing, because the alternative is not appealing.

Will you choose to thrive, or become yet another casualty?

Most people will be stuck in the fear-based doom and gloom mindset, complaining about prices, being a victim and blaming the government, but not you. The entrepreneur in you will take massive action on the things you **can** control. You're a leader, even if you don't know it yet, because leaders lead themselves first, they lead their families away from suffering and in doing so clear the path for others to follow suit.

During the Coronavirus pandemic when businesses were closed, and jobs were lost it felt like everyone around me was feeling the negative effects. I sat back behind closed doors and quietly celebrated my most financially successful year to date in a thriving Network Marketing business. The Network Marketing haters out there would call that taking advantage of people's vulnerability at a difficult time, but I saw an opportunity to help as many families as humanly possible to recognise the joy in earning an income from home and spending time with and providing for their families without the pressures of a boss or a draining commute. I helped men and women to learn new skills and build businesses that would provide for their families for a lifetime, and I'm incredibly proud of that. I'm in the business of giving hope and opportunity to others and so are you. It's a valuable asset and one that will always be in demand.

Running an online business was once a nice little 'top-up', a side hustle, a 'thing on the side', but times have changed. Having an additional income is fast becoming a necessity and what we have here as network marketers is so much more than that. The income from my business quickly surpassed anything I ever earned as a teacher just as soon as I started to take it seriously, and that's the key statement here.

If you treat your business like a side gig, it will pay you like a side gig. If you treat it like the profession that it is, it'll pay you like a profession, and then some. *#nwmrevolution*

I want you to know that with what you have here, you're fully capable of thriving in any circumstance. With the right guidance and the right offer, you're fully capable of setting your family up for the rest of your life. Even when everything else seems to be falling around your ears, you have everything you need to thrive. That's because the two major business types that thrive in financial crises are opportunity-based businesses and education. If you hadn't noticed, Network Marketing happens to be both of those. As an opportunity-based business, we give people the opportunity, the tools, the training and the mentorship to dig themselves out of a dark place. This is powerful because whilst most people are on the **defence** taking the knocks and the struggles, cutting costs and getting by, we network marketers are on the **offence,** we're on the attack and focusing on what we **can** control and helping out as many people as we possibly can along the way. If you choose to, that is.

If you set goals, make a plan and work on executing that plan every day, you'll thrive and you'll help other families to thrive too. This is not about sell, sell, selling your products, it's about helping as many families as humanly possible, which is exactly what business should be about; solving problems and creating solutions for those who need them. Circumstances like these have a habit of either bringing new perspectives or highlighting old perspectives that we should have recognised before. When you focus on helping others, you'll inevitably help yourself. We forget that sometimes.

What people want more than anything is to have control over their own lives, and that's exactly the business we're in. We were built to thrive and with the right strategy in place, thrive we will.

If you choose to allow it, this economic downturn could be the making of you, and the turning point for your family.

Part Two

THE SOLUTION

Starting The Network Marketing Revolution

#NWMRevolution

> **"A Sum can be put right: but only by going back til you find the error and working it afresh from that point, never by simply going on."**
>
> — C.S. LEWIS

> **"We repeat what we don't repair."**
>
> — UNKNOWN

8

THE FREEDOM FRAMEWORK

The Strategic Plate Spinning System

When you envisage someone spinning plates, thoughts of multi-tasking, exhaustion, chaos and stress come to mind. They certainly do for me anyway. You might liken it to being a busy parent, juggling three jobs, managing life and running a home, all the while sweeping the floor with a broom up your... Before learning to earn online I was juggling plates, bowls, cups and the whole damn cutlery drawer. I feel exhausted just thinking about it!

But, if you've ever seen a professional plate-spinning performer, they're not at all frantic. They're calm and focused and do it with finesse and a smug smile. With a specially selected set of plates, patience, skill and lots of practice, over time, they can get their plates to spin on their own with nothing more than a little adjustment here and there, and so can you. In this section, I'll show you how with my 'Strategic Plate Spinning System' aka 'The Freedom Framework'

Part Two is all about learning to select the right plates, and how to skilfully add and spin one plate at a time. None of this standing on one leg and spinning plates on every extremity; chaos and burnout have no place in Network Marketing, or in any online business for that matter. Plate Spinning should be effortless (done with a finesse and a smug smile) Part Two is where we step away from the outdated methods that weren't built for us to thrive in this new evolving economy and step into a new way of earning an income online with ease, excitement and enjoyment as a plate spinning extraordinaire.

The idea is to learn how to add one strategically chosen plate at a time and keep patiently practising until you have all the plates spinning to the point that you could almost walk away. When you've cracked it and they're spinning all by themselves with very little involvement from you, that's what we call automation. The aptly named 'Freedom Framework' will allow you to build a business you no longer have to spend every minute of your day working in and on to make a substantial income.

As far as I can see, so many people fail to make a success of their Network Marketing business because they...

1. Take one look at the plates and poles and decide there and then that they can't do it.
2. Dip their toe in the water and "*give it a try*", (said in my best lame, dithery voice), half-heartedly follow advice then inevitably get distracted and watch their plates wobble off never to be picked up again.
3. Enthusiastically begin but spend ages faffing about with the set-up and choose the 'pretty plates' rather than the practical ones (*i.e. put all their efforts into attractive but pointless activities instead of the stuff that will make them money - then wonder why it's not working*)

4. Start out well, and follow the initial training but start to get disheartened when they realise it's not as easy as it looks. Instead of persevering, they convince themselves that plate spinning was never for them and crawl back into their awkwardly uncomfortable comfort zone and settle for mediocre over-plate spinning stardom.
5. Over enthusiastically throw themselves in headfirst like a bit of a 'know it all', the plates come crashing down around them and they either blame the tools, the plates or the training. Some quickly realise they should probably have listened to the advice they were given by other expert plate spinners; others go off into the world telling everyone that those plate spinning extraordinaire you see online are nothing but fakes and frauds; plate spinning is impossible.

Have you ever walked into a job and known exactly what to do on the first day, week or even month? I know I haven't. I dare say I was a pretty bog-standard teacher for the first year, despite having two degrees, a PGCE and hours of teaching practice under my belt. I learnt on the job and had many a rude awakening along the way. Just like learning to drive a car, you don't just jump in, stall a few times then get out saying we can't do it, that the instructor's crap and the car's broken.

Have you ever watched a toddler learning to walk? Did you see them fall down for the 232nd time and say, *"do you know what, forget it, I'm just gonna crawl through life, the cat does it, and those big people look stupid stuck up on two legs like that anyway*". Of course you haven't (firstly because they probably can't string such a complex, witty sentence together, amusing as that would be) because we were born with huge amounts of resilience and you've chosen to let life chip away at it. Just like our toddler selves, we must take life a step at a time, make mistakes, fall, learn from it and get straight back up. Just like when we learnt to walk, we must hone our skills until we master them, not give up at the first sniff of adversity. This is true of literally all aspects of life and in any profession, yet people walk into Network Marketing thinking they'll start making money instantly then quit within three months because 'it doesn't work'. This has always baffled me. I'm not one for "channelling my inner child" but for Christ's sake, if your one year old self was more resilient than the adult you are now, it's definitely time to give yourself a talking to.

"To achieve real success in our profession is no different from mastering any musical instrument or sport, you have to learn specific skills".

— SIMON CHAN

Sure, some plates might be harder to get spinning than others; I was always terrible at reversing around a corner, hated it and hated my driving instructor for making me do it a million times a lesson, but I accepted that mastering the skill would take patience and practise and when I passed my test with flying colours, I was the happiest seventeen year old alive!

Of course, throughout your journey, it's likely that the odd plate will take a wobble or maybe even fall off completely, but that's OK too. That's life, we just pick it back up and keep going. What's exciting is that skill, patience and resilience pays off, (I mean, I'm not one to brag, but I've been walking, skipping and running around for years thanks to the efforts I put in early on) meaning when you get the balance right in your business, the automation will kick in and you can start to kick back.

Over the course of Part Two, I'll introduce you to each of the plates in turn. Each is an essential part of the overall 'Freedom Framework' and once you've learnt how to spin all these plates on automation, you can add as many additional plates, cups, bowls, forks and spoons as you like - **but not until.** Once you've cracked it, the 'Freedom Framework' has the potential to deliver you as much time, location and financial freedom as you can handle.

A Highly Profitable Business Model & Irresistable Offer
The Secret
Community & Mentorship
The Backup
A Personal Brand & Attentive Audience
The Magic that Many Miss
The Freedom Framework
Strategic Plate Spinning System
Social Media Leverage
The Rocket Fuel
Systems & Automation
The Freedom Formula

The Plates...

1. A Highly Profitable Business Model and Irresistible Offer (The Secret)
2. Personal Brand and Attentive Audience (The Magic that Many Miss)
3. Systems and Automation (The Freedom Formula)
4. Social Media Leverage (The Rocket Fuel)
5. Community and Mentorship (The Backup)

9

A HIGHLY PROFITABLE BUSINESS MODEL AND IRRESISTIBLE OFFER

The Secret

Your offer, what you're selling, is arguably the most important plate of all, because, without an irresistible offer that solves your audience's most pressing problems, you'll always have strong opposition from those with offers that do. Whether it be a potentially life-changing product or a profitable business opportunity, your offer needs to be so irresistible to them that they love it, want it and need it **now**! And if you're planning to achieve some of those ridiculously audacious goals you set yourself, you need it to be profitable for you too.

You did set those goals in Chapter 6 right? I asked you to download the **#nwmrevolution** workbook, prioritise your values, write your goals and calculate how much you'll need to earn each month to fund the lifestyle you've planned out for yourself. If you haven't, then please, do yourself a favour and go do that now. I've been the person who skips over the activities in a book, a million times over because *"oh I don't need to do that"*. Shall I tell you what happened when I skipped the activities? Nothing. Nothing happened! Because loading your brain up with information like a squirrel cramming nuts in his cheeks means nothing if you don't do anything with it. If information was all we ever needed to be successful in life and business, every single one of us would be insanely happy and rolling around in our millions, because in this digital age we're overloaded with the stuff, every second of every day. Implementation and action aka 'doing the work' are the crucial elements that take that information from being about someone else's success, to being about **you and yours.** Remember what I said right at the beginning of the book?

You can't complain about the success you never had; from the work, you didn't do.

#nwmrevolution

Go do the task and come back!

www.nwmrevolution.com/resources

So, you've done that? Great! What we need to do now is to question whether your current offer and the company you're affiliated with are aligned with the big goal. Is it going to allow you to replace your income or buy you that Malibu beach house? Does it have the potential to make that monthly amount you worked out? If yes, why aren't you there yet? What's not quite adding up? Refer back to the Trifecta of Triumph in Chapter Five if you have to.

Does your current offer have the potential to bring all the time and financial freedom you need to do the things you listed? How long is that likely to take you? How many products would you have to sell each month and how much work are you going to have to put in to get you there? Are you prepared to do that work, or does that mean missing out on time with your family and not aligning with those highest priorities? Only you can answer these questions because only you know what you're doing right now and how your current offer's going down. I secretly suspect there's room for improvement or you're seeking a change of trajectory altogether though, if you've felt compelled to pick up this book.

So, so many people say things to me at this stage like, 'but it's not really about the money', I think I probably said that too, but income almost always comes into the equation somewhere whether we like to admit it or not. No, perhaps money doesn't always buy happiness, but it does buy you freedom of choice, it buys further options, and it opens doors and opportunities that might not otherwise be available to you and having those can bring contentment and peace of mind even when there are other difficulties in life. So, making sure you're working with a business model that's profitable is almost certainly high up there on the agenda somewhere, regardless of your highest values.

When I first started looking for an alternative income to my teaching career, my highest priority was time freedom and flexibility, because as I mentioned earlier, my dad had just been diagnosed with dementia and the job just wasn't allowing me the time or flexibility needed to support my mum with his care. I also needed whatever I was working on to consistently cover or exceed my existing salary, because I had a mortgage and responsibilities like most of us and I wasn't prepared to take a pay cut.

What I found with many of the business models I looked at was that they involved either sacrificing my time or level of income. I wasn't expecting a quick fix or to earn money for nothing, don't get me wrong. I knew I'd have to put in the work, but I needed it to be much more flexible and, on my terms, and finding something like that was tricky.

At that time, Network Marketing wasn't even on my radar. In my mind, back then, it was for annoying people who wanted to earn a bit of money on the side selling random stuff to their friends and family. What I was looking for was a profession, a business I could be proud of and call my own and I just couldn't see Network Marketing producing anywhere near the levels of income I was looking for. How very wrong I was. I write this book today to dispel that very myth.

You might well be feeling the same way, you might have found yourself hitting a ceiling in your Network Marketing business, struggling to make sales or perhaps the amount of effort you're having to put in just isn't translating into money in the bank, and for that reason, you might be doubting your place in the industry altogether. Maybe that's why you picked up this book, as a last-ditch attempt at making a breakthrough.

You're absolutely in the right place, I hope you know that by now, but just so I can be sure those doubts are well squashed, incinerated and destroyed forever, let's look at some of the alternatives.

If not Network Marketing, then what?

The first thing I considered was another job, a different career. But I just wasn't inspired by a single thing I saw on the million job sites I'd signed up to, and the thought of having to sit through another interview and be judged by someone with half my qualifications and experience on how much I deserved to be paid made me feel sick to my stomach. Just like the smell of the warm tupperware boxes I'd eaten from for so many years. Who'd have thought that being able to eat my lunch from a plate everyday would become one of the perks I'd appreciate most about working from home. Ah, the little things.

You've also no doubt heard the 'ugh it's a pyramid scheme' thing too many times to mention, and you know as well as I do that the biggest scam out there is the pyramid called the j.o.b. A neat little triangle where the CEO sits counting his money at the top above the managers, supervisors and then the general dog's body staff at the bottom. Most people stay in a job like this for years hoping they might eventually climb the ladder and enjoy the odd pay rise along the way, then call Network Marketing a pyramid scheme and a scam, laughable really. Most people never have the opportunity to reach that CEO level like we do, and even if you *are* the CEO, you're still working your life away until 65 or whatever unearthly age it is now before you can retire and start enjoying your time-freedom.

Network Marketing is one of the few industries that make CEO-level salaries available to everyone. We all start on a level playing field, we all have access to the same opportunities, training, products etc, and the only person stopping you from reaching the top is you. The prospect of life-changing legacy income for everyone is real, yet so many people don't challenge themselves enough to take it, and instead cling on to their standard issue j.o.b. security blanket.

Be honest with yourself, can you see a job of any kind, even if it offered more flexible hours, creating the lifestyle you have set out for yourself in your **#nwmrevolution** workbook? And does it align with your highest priorities, like time with your family, or travel for example? Maybe not, and maybe that's why you started a Network Marketing business to begin with. Maybe this book is the push you're looking for to exit that cycle.

Maybe you considered starting a traditional business. Being your own boss has its advantages for sure, but also comes with a lot of responsibility and, depending on the type of business, investment risk. If you were to open up a cake shop, or a yoga studio for example, there would be physical assets to buy and costs to cover like a lease, equipment, staff etc. Whilst many are successful, I recently read that most traditional businesses shouldn't expect to make a profit for at least 3-5 years! Sure, it may well be something you've always wanted to do, a passion project, who doesn't want to earn doing something they love? But the excitement soon wears off when the honeymoon period is over, it's not paying the bills or you're having to put long day and night shifts in just to make it work. Is your passion project going to bring you the levels of income you need each month for the foreseeable future or are you just going to end up trading time for money again? These are important questions to ask yourself.

My dad and brother had the freedom of their own businesses for years, they worked for themselves on a 'self-employed' basis and their customers paid them directly. They got to choose what they charged which was great, but if they weren't working, they weren't earning and if they wanted to earn more, they had to work more, and they were lucky enough to always have the work available to them.

A lovely lady I know is a self-employed therapist and can charge a good hourly rate for her services. She's always fully booked which is great, but that means her income is capped at the number of hours she's physically able to work. Again, if she's not working, she's not earning so things like illness can be a problem as there's no time leverage here.

Another good friend of mine is somewhat of a 'Del Boy' of Only Fools and Horses fame in terms of fingers in pies and the many businesses he's had. (It's an old 80's UK comedy show about a hilarious Cockney Wheeler Dealer if you've not heard of it) From a failed Chinese supermarket to those horrible little fish that eat the skin on your feet, he entertains us all with his crazy business venture stories; you name it, he's tried it. Until the last few years that is, when he discovered Network Marketing. When someone with many, many years' experience in traditional business drops them all to plant their flag within our industry, we should take note. And he's not the first.

> **"If I had to do it all over again, rather than build an old-style type of business I would have started building a Network Marketing Business"**
>
> — ROBERT KIYOSAKI

> **"If I was given the chance to start all over again, I'd choose Network Marketing"**
>
> — BILL GATES

"The best investment I've ever made"

— WARREN BUFFET

Recent events have seen the need for many traditional business owners to pivot and take their offline businesses online. The coaching industry, for example, is huge at the moment, and my therapist friend had to quickly learn how to use video software and start coaching her clients from a distance. This simple transition brought a new element of location freedom which was great, but she was still restricted to that hourly rate and still stuck exchanging time for money with a capped income.

Some coaches offer group sessions or training which means that time can be leveraged, and a higher hourly rate can be earned for working with more than one person at once. This all sounds great, but having worked with a lot of coaches, burnout is very common. I suspect this might be down to the fact that competition in online coaching is fierce and standing out amongst the noise relies on you constantly going the extra mile and being that something different. Being a one-man band also means you're wearing all the hats. Until you're earning enough to hire staff or additional support, as an independent online business owner you're your own sales department, marketing department and finance department. You'd also be your own legal team, social media manager, design creative, not to mention IT specialist and tech builder. And that's before you even start the actual coaching or whatever it is you do to make money. This all comes with a steep learning curve and no manual, which inevitably leads to investing in further support or other coaches to guide you in the right direction. Network Marketing is one of few industries that offers mentorship, training and support as part of the deal at no cost to you and is the perfect introduction to entrepreneurship for this very reason. It's amazing the number of people I speak to who tell me that Network Marketing was their first, and very valuable experience of running a business.

Some online business owners create and sell their own digital products. This can be set up in a similar way to the coaching idea, only you're selling digital assets for others to utilise, rather than your time.

Perhaps you have a specific skill that you could teach others, or maybe you're knowledgeable about a particular subject and could create an online course, an E-Book or Instructions, workbooks or 'how to' guides. What do you know that you could teach others? Is there an audience for this kind of information? The answer is most certainly yes.

You can earn a steady passive income by creating your own courses or downloadables, but again, without help and support it's a steep and sometimes costly learning curve. The support to get started is out there, but at a cost, and what will your return on investment look like? How many of these downloadables would you have to sell to make your money back, and then make a profit?

DIY courses and downloadables also tend to sell at a much lower cost than if you were to give up your time and energy to help individuals specifically, so you'd have been confident you could sell a large number to make any kind of profit, and that means building a good, loyal audience of buyers. If you already have said audience, then this could be a nice supplementary income for you.

Alternatively, (or additionally) you could partner with an existing organisation that already has a proven business model for you to follow. They already have products that people want, need and love, all you need to do is plug in and learn how to promote them. The business itself is still your own, but you're not 100% responsible for every aspect like you would be with most other online businesses and this reduces the amount of time, pressure and responsibility. You're not having to wear all the hats because a lot of it is already **done for you**, similar to what you would find with a franchise model. This is a huge bonus when you're short on time or just starting out. You're simply given the tools and the training on how to best promote it and then get paid a commission as an affiliate when a customer makes a purchase.

Do you recognise this business model? That's right, that's all Network Marketing is, it's selling other people's proven, tried and tested products (that people already need, want and love) instead of your own.

Network Marketing really isn't any different to how others run their businesses online, yet people treat it like it's not a 'real' business or like some sort of inferior relative. In reality, it's no different, other than, the probability of success is likely to be much higher because the business model and offer are already proven, tried and tested.

It's only those who use shoddy, spammy sales tactics that make it appear to be less than professional, and putting a stop to that behaviour and smartening up the act is what **The Network Marketing Revolution *#nwmrevolution*** is all about. We should be as loud and proud about our profession as the next person because our offers stand up against (and in many cases beat, hands-down) any other online offer out there with a fraction of the time and effort involved. Why be a busy fool? Remember, when you treat your business like a profession, it'll pay you like a profession and others will respect you as the professional that you are. Whether you promote your own offer, or someone else's, it really doesn't matter, what matters is that the business model is profitable and in line with your future income goals and values.

As a side note here, I've created my own digital assets and sold them and I've also partnered with other organisations and promoted their products too. Although creating and selling your own products feels special and brings an element of pride because it's your baby, it was also much more time consuming, stressful and the profit was minimal when compared with partnering and promoting something that already exists using a system that was done for me and methods that were proven, tried and tested. There really is no point in trying to reinvent the wheel.

Partnering was by far the simplest and most highly profitable, and definitely created the most time freedom for me. This now equates to over 95% of my income.

That said, adding an affiliate offer and partnering with a company to add value, and an additional passive income to an already successful online (or offline for that matter) business is a smart and highly efficient way to boost your legacy income. Remember what top entrepreneurs 'Gates, Buffet and Kiyosaki said earlier? With a ready primed, loyal following, simply adding an additional offer to your arsenal can be highly lucrative. Many business owners fear that adding a Network Marketing offer would cheapen or jeopardise their existing offer, for the many reasons and misconceptions discussed in Part One. On the contrary, when you're operating as a professional and recommending an offer you love and trust to an already loyal audience, you really have nothing to lose and everything to gain. Just as you'd recommend your favourite restaurant to a friend, you're simply just sharing your love of something that could benefit them too.

As far as trust is concerned, I can't stress how important it is to choose a well-established company to partner with. By well-established I mean a company that gives you peace of mind, has stood the test of time and has preferably shown itself to thrive through previous economic downturns. I would recommend ten solid years of successful history at an absolute minimum, but preferably more. I'm a huge advocate of finding the right partner and planting your flag firmly in the ground. None of this, flitting from one 'next big thing' to the another like a fly on a buffet. If you're always jumping from one thing to the next, how can you possibly have time to grow roots and the foundations of a long-standing and successful career?

When it comes to partnering, the level of income achievable versus time spent earning it will depend on the type of company you choose to partner with. And amongst the vast variety, there are two primary types for you to choose from. Those that sell low-priced products and those that sell higher-priced products.

The difference is quite straightforward. Low-priced products cost less, so the commission paid to you is less. To be highly profitable and meet the needs and requirements of your newly laid out goals, you'd need to either sell a large number of these products yourself or rely on recruiting and maintaining a team beneath you to also make sales, which can be frustrating and time-consuming. Higher priced products cost more, so pay higher commissions to you when sold. You don't have to sell as many to make the same amount of income, which means you could probably make these sales profitably yourself (direct) without having to rely on recruiting others.

That said, if you choose to build a team beneath you too, additional commissions from them would be an added bonus. Since you also don't 'need' to make as many sales to hit your goals, there's much less pressure to sell, sell, sell and you can be much smarter and more strategic and selective about who you work with.

Some people believe that it's harder to sell a higher-priced product than it is to sell a lower-priced product, but this is simply a matter of perspective. Those who believe this, have probably been trying to sell their higher-priced products to the wrong audience. You wouldn't expect to see success selling Cartier watches in the queue at Primani for example, would you. Don't get me wrong, I love a Primani bargain as much as the next person, but the shoppers are just not your average high-ticket audience. To successfully sell a high-value product, you need to know where your audience is most likely to hang out, and then promote your offer there. When you nail your target market, it takes the same amount of energy to sell a higher-priced product as it does to sell a lower-priced one. You're just selling to different people, that's literally all it takes.

If you were an independent estate agent for example, would you rather sell ten £100k houses for 5% commission on each to make a 50k profit, or **one** £1million house for the same 5%

commission which is also a 50k profit. I know which I'd choose. Your ability to sell one over the other is all a matter of skillset and mindset; things that can be easily mastered.

The process and the amount of time spent on each sale are the same, so when you only need to sell ONE product to make the same amount of commission, it takes much less effort and frees up much more of your time.

The process of selling a house, or anything for that matter, is the same regardless of how much it costs, it's just the audience and approach that's different and that's something I can teach you.

Before we talk more about the financials, it is of course also really important that your values are also in alignment with the company you're partnered with, and that you're passionate about your offer. Nobody can make a good living selling stuff they're not that into. Your passion and enthusiasm shine through when you talk about an offer that lights you up, and that's the magic that brings sales. It's easy to recommend something you stand behind and love and your customers are more likely to want, need and love it too. To be fair, in my experience, most Network Marketing products are of pretty good quality, but to be successful in business and to meet those life goals, there's so much more to it than liking or loving what you sell. You need to love, live and breathe it. You also need to be sure your business will be profitable without having to work your bits off day and night to get there, and that's why I advocate the promotion of a small number of higher-priced items over stressing yourself out mass selling lower priced ones. Call me lazy if you like, but personally I'd just rather do less work.

Now go back to the big life goals you set yourself in your **#nwmrevolution** workbook. For this example, we're going to assume that your dream lifestyle is going to need around £10,000 per month ($12k) to maintain. The house, the car, the holidays/holiday home, the hobbies, the luxuries, retiring your partner, the extra experiences for the kids. I did say to think big, maybe £10k a month won't be enough?

Take this example and a goal of £10k per month.

(Income/Business Model One)

It took Caroline 4-5 years to recruit a team of 700 distributors in her MLM and on her best months she would average £100,000 in product sales. **She earned 5% of that volume which = £5,000.** To reach her £10k commission goal in a month Caroline would need to double the number of sales made in her team. Caroline would find it difficult to make those sales herself every month and must rely on a large team to sell a small number each.

For her team members, this isn't lucrative unless they recruit a large team themselves too, which makes it more difficult to keep them motivated and on board. Caroline has to work hard to maintain a team at that level, and at the end of each month feels the need to push hard to maintain rank. The pressure from above forces her to pressurise others into sell, sell, selling or convincing them to purchase more. This all leads to higher attrition rates.

Disclaimer: The examples used in this book are just that, examples of what's possible. They do not relate to any particular company or compensation plan.

Does this sound familiar? Do you feel **you** could do this EVERY. SINGLE. MONTH to maintain rank and that level of commission? It's possible. People do. Just like Caroline.

Do you find yourself spending the last week of the month desperately trying to meet target and avoid being de-ranked, only to find the following week you're back to zero and have to do it aaaaallll over again the next month? I've lost count of the number of people who've told me that they bought products themselves just to meet target, maintain rank and keep their benefits.

Take a minute and think about that, is this the makings of a profitable business model? This might all sound very normal to you but it's alien to me and I for one have never partnered with a company who set targets, let alone one that would consider de-ranking me. Companies that don't put pressure on you to be a ruthless sales vulture do exist, and they appreciate and thank you for every sale you put their way, by way of timely commission payments straight into your account. This allows you the breathing space to figure out a way of working that suits you and your lifestyle. You know as well as I do, when you start from scratch it's a steep learning curve, you make mistakes and you learn as you go along. I cringe when I think of some of the first posts I put out, but learnt and improved with every single, cheesy one of them. When you're given breathing space to learn and develop at your own pace, rather than rushed into pushing out posts, hounding friends and meeting targets, you'll come across much more authentically (which in itself will attract more attention) and build much stronger foundations upon which you'll build a thriving business **your** way.

Here's a slightly different example. **(Income/Business Model Two)**

When Sarah started her Network Marketing business, it took her a few months to make her first sale, but when she did, on her first two sales she made a commission of £1700 on each one.

2 x £1700.00 = **£3400.00**

She then ranked up so the amount of commission per sale paid directly to her increased.

(She can never be de-ranked as this is not company policy)

Her next sale paid a commission of **£2250.00** and she ranked up again.

Her next two sales paid a commission of £2850.00 each

2 x £2850.00 = **£5700.00**

£3400.00 + £2250.00 + £5700.00 = **£11,350.00 commission in 5 sales.**

(Approx $13,700.00 or €12,800.00)

Sarah exceeded the £10k month goal she set herself by making just five sales.

Disclaimer: The examples used in this book are just that, examples of what's possible. They do not relate to any particular company or compensation plan.

Sarah was selling much higher priced products as you can see, (around £10,000 per sale in this example) but as a result, didn't have to sell nearly as many, and was able to make these five sales herself without relying on a team. If she had a team, any commissions for sales made by them would have been paid out in addition to this.

What's more, Sarah had no monthly qualifications or targets to meet which meant she could learn in her own sweet time without being penalised for her mistakes. It didn't matter if she didn't meet her personal goal of 10k in one month, because she could simply keep going until she did, building her business over time.

The difference between the high and low priced product examples is quite unbelievable isn't it. Too good to be true, some might say. But it's still Network Marketing and it's no different to the property example I gave earlier, it's just a case of opening your eyes to new ways of doing things and understanding that the adjustment is in your approach and the audience you're marketing to, which is something we'll cover in the next chapter. People often overthink and over complicate these things, but when it comes down to it, when your offer solves your audience's most pressing problems, they'll want, need and love it so much that they'll approach you, not the other way around! If you found your dream house online and it was in your price range, would you wait patiently for the estate agent to contact you, or would you get on the phone and make an appointment right away? It's no different. Positioning is everything. If you hang around in the right places looking/being irresistible for long enough, you'll soon get snapped up.

REVOLUTIONARY TIP

Selling Higher Priced Items = Higher Commissions and More Profit in Less Time.

But not everyone is in this to achieve big goals or make big lifestyle changes, I understand that. I just wanted to demonstrate that if you are, then the opportunities are out there for the taking. If you're perfectly happy with your life and career and your goal is simply to create an additional income on the side, that's great too. If you're partnered with a company that will help you achieve those goals, go for it! We all have different aspirations in life, analysing and strategising means matching **your** income/business model to **your** life goals. You do you! The following chapters will help you make the most of what you've got and smarten up your strategy so that the income, at whatever level you're looking for, flies in with ease and enjoyment.

Just don't fall into the trap of settling for mediocrity because those big numbers sound scary. Self-belief is everything. Until a few years ago I never dared to dream. I'd settled and accepted what I considered to be the cards I'd been dealt. But as soon as I opened my eyes to what was possible and I saw everyday people achieving what I'd previously considered unachievable, I jumped straight on it. If they could make those big numbers, why couldn't I?

If you're feeling deflated, fatigued, bedraggled and defeated, chances are you've been trying so hard for so long that you feel all is lost. That's what happens when your income/business model and/or strategy doesn't match your income goal. It's a simple case of mismatched expectations. It's easy for your drive, determination and enthusiasm to wane when your results don't match your efforts. What you need to do now is use what you learn here in this book to figure out how to match them up. Will you lower your goals and expectations or upgrade your income/business model and strategy?

"Do not lower your goals to the level of your abilities. Instead, raise your abilities to the height of your goals."

— SWAMI VIVEKANANDA

REVOLUTIONARY TASK

Return to your **#nwmrevolution** workbook and revisit your numbers. Knowing what you know now and what's achievable. Would you change anything? Did you find yourself with some more extravagant, audacious goals? Good! For some of you, making just one high-profit sale per month might be enough to pay the bills or replace your existing salary, but why settle for one?

You can download all the Revolutionary Tasks here at

www.nwmrevolution.com/resources

For the more sceptical of you out there (there was no one more sceptical than me when I discovered this 'too good to be true' goldmine of an industry believe me) perhaps you need to process it a little more. You'll also find some journal-style questions in your workbook which will help you navigate through what we've covered in this last chapter.

KEY CHAPTER TAKEAWAYS

- When approached with consistency and dedicated action, it's thought that the probability of success in Network Marketing is likely to be much higher than in a standard online business because the business model and offer are already proven, tried and tested.
- The level of income achievable versus time spent earning it will depend on the type of company you choose to partner with.
- Selling Higher Priced Items = Higher Commissions and More Profit in Less Time.
- It takes the same amount of effort to sell a higher priced product as it does to sell a lower priced product, the adjustment is in your approach and the audience you're marketing to.
- When your chosen company/business model and marketing strategy doesn't match the requirements of your future income goal you can become deflated and fatigued. It's important to find a suitable match if you are to reach that goal.

Although I'd highly recommend reading on to get a fuller picture of how achievable this can all be for you, I also recognise that some of you won't be able to rest and will need clarity on this right now. If that's you, you can visit www.nwmrevolution.com/call to book a free 15-minute clarity call where you can ask all the questions you need.

10

PERSONAL BRANDING AND AN ATTENTIVE AUDIENCE

The Magic that Many Miss

'It's a Network **Marketing** Business,
not a Network **Selling** Business'
#nwmrevolution

"The aim of marketing is make selling superfluous"

— PETER DRUCKER

This next plate is essential, and not getting this right is probably the single biggest mistake I see people make, and a huge contributory factor in terms of struggling to make sales. Here are a few examples of things I see network marketers do time and time again... either

1. They stick their company's product offer template out on social media with a bit of info in the hope someone spots it and buys. Sometimes they'll personalise it a little with some text, but not always.
2. They make generic statements and assumptions about their audience's problems on social media (because it's a mixed audience and they don't really know about the backgrounds of each one individually). i.e. needing to lose weight, get fit etc. Or, they cold message individuals without knowing their background *"Are you looking to lose weight?"* (I've seen that one go down like a shit sandwich let me tell you) then proceed to insist that they need their product/opportunity in their lives without actually knowing their customer's background, needs or wants. A wild stab in the dark if you will.[1]
3. They try to convince people that they have a problem they don't even know they have in an attempt to sell their product to them. (*"Omg really? I didn't even realise I had a double chin until you pointed it out!"*) Dodgy territory this one - but it happens.

Once again, if this is you, I forgive you. We can be friends (but only because you've probably been taught to do this stuff by someone who should know better). All of this, random 'targeting' and stuffing of square pegs into round holes is not customer focused or an effective strategy. It stinks of me, me, me.

How can **I** make a sale?

What can **I** get out of this?

It's the sell, sell, sell mentality that is brought about by the desperation to meet month-end targets, and once again, that's not your fault. The system encourages this crap. Many companies encourage you to lead with the product and be the face of their brand. It looks good on them, and it makes it more difficult for you to leave and start something different if you've plastered how amazing they are all over your news feed (because that's what they said works)!

I want you to imagine walking into a shopping mall where all the shops look exactly the same, and they all sell exactly the same thing, for the same price. No labels, no fancy signage, no packaging or pretty paper bags etc. Why would you choose to buy from one shop over another?

When you're leading with your company and your company's brand on social media, that's exactly what you're doing. There are thousands of other distributors out there doing exactly the same thing, posting the same posts, with the same products, for the same price as you. You're in direct competition with them, not to mention all the other internet noise. Why would I buy my essence of fairy fluff from you when I could just as easily buy it (or some other equally amazing, mythical fluff) from somewhere/someone else? When you're simply pushing your company's brand and products it's totally generic and you may as well be stood handing out leaflets in the street. There's nothing unique about you or any of the other distributors sharing the company's offer and I could just as easily spend three seconds Googling and have the fairy fluff delivered to my doorstep the very next day, from some other random internet stranger; the transaction is meaningless.

If you do what everyone else does, you'll get what they get; which is not what they make out they're getting half the time (see Chapter Four on Porky Pies (Lies)). Answer me this, are the leaders in your company sharing the same offer graphics and generic templates given to you to share? No. They're too busy building their own personal brand because they know that's the most effective way. These generic templates are made for lazy marketers who lack the imagination and foresight to stray away from conventional norms and do things their own way. That's not the makings of a successful business owner. Have the courage to play by your own rules and put your own personal stamp on your business. That's right, **'your'** business.

Sure, it might be quicker and easier for you to use the company's branding material and stick a few things out there to make a few extra quid before the end of the month, and that might work for you in the short term, but in the long term, it's counterproductive, you're not creating a memorable experience and that our super savvy customers crave that these days.

Something that drives me crazy is when people say *'check out **'our'** latest XYZ offer'*. No, just no. They're not **'(y)our'** products at all, they're your company's products and it's your company's brand, and they've got you brainwashed and doing their donkey work for them. What if they took those products off sale tomorrow? In fact, what if they went bust and dropped off the face of the planet or made some silly publicity mistake and lost all credibility and custom overnight. Then where would you be, would you still be promoting **'our'** products? This is **your** business, so take the wheel, stop limiting yourself and drive it to success **your** way.

The most effective way is to build a Personal Brand that revolves around **you**. Personal branding is about defining and sharing what you stand for as an individual and is a culmination of the experiences, skills and values that differentiate you from others. In essence, it's everything that makes you, you!

Why is leading with a personal brand important? Because shit happens, companies go bust, you change your mind about stuff, you pivot, and you'll decide to do things differently as you grow along your journey and that's totally fine. When you're just out there being you, as your own personal brand, you can do that and nobody will be any the wiser, you can diversify, have multiple income streams and sell what the hell you like. People will follow and buy from **you** because you're **you**, they believe in you and they trust your opinions. People don't generally give a crap about your products, your company or the compensation plan in the first instance, what they're attracted to initially is you, they like how you come across, admire what you stand for and often wish they were a little bit more like you too. Think about the millions of people that buy everything and anything the Kardashian's release, it's not because the top quality, irresistible products they sell (can you even name one?), it's because they've been endorsed by a personal brand that so many people love and respect. I'm not saying you need to be an all out influencer or anything, far from it, but there's something to be said for becoming an inspiration to a select bunch of people in your own tiny corner of the internet. You don't even have to be a raging success, you just need to be you, relatable to people like you and prepared to speak up about what you love and what you believe in.

It's so easy to get caught up in our own lives and what *we* need, but what we actually need to do is bring the customer or potential new team member back to the forefront and remember that pleasing them is what will draw them in and keep them coming back for more. I'll share some strategies to do that shortly.

I have an online friend who's one of those annoyingly fit, energetic people. She manages to make me feel like an utter failure each morning as I start the scroll and realise that she's already been on live, run 5k, downed a kale and cucumber smoothie and is now running a fifteen-minute live yoga class, all before I've even put the kettle on. This online friend also sells workout leggings, and I bought some. Not because I needed any, or because I couldn't just go and buy myself a very similar pair down at Asda, but because a little piece of me thought that if I bought her leggings, I would become a little bit more like her; I'd suddenly find the energy and ability to jump out of bed and go for a run every morning. Of course, I know that's totally ridiculous but that's how she made me **feel** (and yes I can confirm, the leggings didn't work, what a scam. Paaah!). I love that she makes her fitness a priority, I love that she eats healthily and promotes physical and mental well-being. We actually have a lot in common despite my clear inadequacies, and that's why we follow each other.

This isn't a show she puts on to make sales either, my annoyingly energetic friend is actually just like that in real life (yes we've met) and is also your average everyday human. She just gets online, no makeup, hair scraped back, warts and all and gets it done, just like we all wish we could do. On the days she just can't be arsed, she tells us so, because that's real life - but she still cracks on, hits the live button and does it anyway. And that's relatable, authentic and aspirational. She doesn't then ram her products down our throats in an effort to make some quick cash. She casually mentions them and shares a link while her legs are akimbo in the air a la *'what do you think to me new leggings eh?'* styleee.

My point here is that, to stand out, you need to be the shop in the mall that offers comfy sofas, snacks and friendly conversation. Be the shop that goes above and beyond by making customers feel comfortable in their own skin, valued and special. In fact, be so far removed from being a shop at all that people drop by for a social and leave with a smile, feeling appreciated and having learned something, even if they didn't spend a penny. If they did, bonus. They might not remember exactly what they bought, but they'll remember **you**, and how you made them **feel,** and **that** is why they'll come back.

The most important thing to remember is that we're 'Network Marketers' **not** Network Sellers.

There's a fundamental difference between 'sales' and 'marketing' and it's the difference between a warm hug and a cold shoulder.

Marketing builds awareness around your brand (that's you and what you stand for) and attracts ideal customers and team members that are excited and ready to buy.

The **sale** is (supposed to be) the bit that follows, where an actual exchange of money/products and service takes place.

Our job as marketers is to position ourselves (notice that I said ourselves and not our products) in a way that attracts the attention of our ideal team members, rouses curiosity and encourages them to dig deeper and ask for more information. When your marketing is on point, selling becomes a mere conversation rather than an act of persuasion, because you've already got to know, like and trust us as individuals. The decision for the customer then becomes an absolute no-brainer because we've also consistently drip-fed sufficient breadcrumbs into the mix to make them hungry for what we sell.

Marketing with a personal brand isn't about expecting to make sales with a post or two, it's about playing the long game, building a reputation as someone who adds value, can help others solve problems, is relatable and can be trusted.

In a recent research paper called 'Zero Moments of Truth' a Google thought leader discovered that once people had around eleven interactions with a brand, they were considerably more likely to buy from them. Eleven! People buy into people and feelings, not things; simply throwing your products out there and hoping people will buy just won't cut it anymore.

REVOLUTIONARY TIP

Going straight in for the sale without building a relationship, awareness and excitement with your marketing is like trying to get someone into bed before you've even so much as participated in small talk or bought them a drink.

(Then again, I've heard that works on some dating apps, so if you're happy to trawl the net and aren't afraid of brutal rejection, go for your life!)

In Chapter Seven we spoke about the current state of the economy. According to top entrepreneurial advisor Scott Oldford, one of the most valuable assets you can own in a recession is a personal brand. Think about it, nobody can take away who you are and what you stand for. In times of uncertainty, people are looking for someone to follow, to look up to. Be that person and show them the way. By helping others, you'll inevitably be helping yourself.

If you choose to separate yourself from the crowd, do things differently and build your own personal brand, you'll find yourself with your own tribe of people who hang onto your every word, love what you stand for and buy everything you recommend. When you use your uniqueness to draw those people away from the generic online noise to become part of 'your gang', they'll become customers and team members for life.

But what if I'm a bit of an introvert or just don't want to put my face out there?

Anyone who's seen me talk on stage will probably have me labelled as some kind of extrovert. So let's get this straight, I'm not. Far from it. If I can put my face out there, you can.

Weirdly, I'm actually more comfortable on stage with a microphone than I am chatting in a room of people. I've always been quite quiet and I'm naturally quite small in stature, so I've never really cared for fighting for a piece of attention and have always been much more of a listener.

I was a painfully shy child and was so petrified of talking to people that when I started school, I cried every day for about 6 months. My mum used to have to get on her little shopper bike and cycle four miles to school and four miles back, every lunchtime just so we could have a cuddle and I could practise my speech. Yes, at 5 years old I was practising a speech! And this was it...

"Hello, I'm Samantha, do you want to be my friend?"

I think I probably only tried it the once, and that poor girl in her matching snowflake hat and gloves was as terrified of me as I was of her.

I was half the size of all the other kids and with sparrows' kneecaps, huge red cheeks and a fringe that started at the back of my head, I was the perfect 'rag doll' for all the other kids. I spoke to no one and they pulled me around like their little play thing. I was a tiny, timid little mouse, afraid of everything and everyone.

Six years of primary school went by and I finally started to find my voice, but not speaking... singing! I bloody loved it! I was **'that'** overly enthusiastic child in the choir that you see on hilarious videos from the 80s (enjoying themselves a bit too much). I didn't talk much, but I could belt out every song from that 'Come and Praise' hymn book!

And that was the start of something amazing. Despite still always being the quiet one in the corner, I actually went on to perform on many stages, first singing and later compering and speaking. Had I suddenly become an extrovert? No. I'm still very, very much that little timid mouse inside.

So how have I managed to put myself out there, build a personal brand and tribe of loyal followers? This is the thing you see, most people think that being an extrovert means you're confident and being an introvert means you lack confidence.

But that's not true.

I don't lack confidence, and neither do you. There will be circumstances where you'll feel uncomfortable, and times when you're as confident as they come. It's not down to being a confident person, it's down to the situation you find yourself in. It's actually about competence, not confidence, and how do you become more competent at something? By doing it, again, and again, and again.

Once you start putting your face out there, your confidence will soar, introvert or not. We make the mistake of comparing ourselves and thinking we're inferior to those people who go about being loud and gregarious, but sometimes people talk alot to hide their lack of confidence. Have you ever considered that? You don't need to be loud or in everyone's faces to attract attention, you just need to be you, honest and relatable.

I'm confident because I'm 'competent' in my knowledge of this industry. Working online is perfect for me because:

1. I get to control how much time I spend in the company of others and how much of 'me' I give (and how much I keep for my loved ones).
2. I still get to share my point of view without having to shout over everyone else, because I'm able to specifically target the people who I already know are going to be interested in what I have to say (more on that later).
3. I can choose the medium in which I want to share my message. I enjoy writing and I **love** that audio has become so popular, because talking to yourself is easy and I don't have to be there squirming when you're listening to it.
4. If I want to share a video and my face, I get to choose how, when, what to say and where I share it. If I'm not happy I can delete it afterwards.

It has to be said though, that despite my initial discomfort, my videos and video trainings tend to go down pretty well and the most common feedback I get is that I come across as very real and relatable (an important point to take note of for later). Another important point to remember is that I can just record these videos on my own, just me, myself and I, when the mood takes me. There's no pressure, no competition and actually, once you've done it a few times, it's much less of a big deal. There's no better way to build trust and a loyal audience than by showing your face on video.

You see, confidence is not about bouncing into a room (or onto the internet) trying to be bigger, better and louder than everyone else. It's about having control of your own circumstances, knowing how to make best use of your talents and knowing that you don't need that attention or validation to feel good about yourself; but that sharing what you know can be really rewarding, especially when it can have such a huge impact on others.

We live in such a loud, fast-paced world where everyone is shouting over each other to be heard, but not actually listening. So, when you're different, genuine and humble, you stand out a mile from the rest and the right people will be attracted to you.

Our industry is renowned for people barging their way into your world and your inbox shouting 'buy my shit' 'buy my shit' like some kind of fruit and veg seller.

But you know what's made me successful? I was just me. I didn't do any shouting. I was just genuine and honest, and helped people out by sharing my learnings and pointing them in the right direction.

I didn't have to push, or sell, sell, sell, because I was quietly confident that when they got to **know** me, **like** me and **trust** me, then they'd inevitably want to work with me at some point when they were ready.

And they did! I get to teach a whole bunch of new people to become confident, honest, genuine businessmen and women now too, which makes it even more of a blessing.

If you're tired of shouting to be heard, stop. With a personal brand you can attract business just by being yourself. You don't have to follow the crowd, or your upline and you don't have to push your products under people's noses to be seen. Feel confident enough to make your own judgments, be humble and trust that you might not know everything yet, but you know how to be you, and that's enough.

I want you to walk away from here feeling relieved that you can stop trying so hard to be who you **think** you need to be to make money online and just be you, we'll line the rest of your ducks up together over the next chapters.

But my life is so dull, who'd want to follow me?

If you're anything like me, when I first started out, I insisted that there was literally nothing unique about me. I couldn't for the life of me think why anyone would be interested in what I'd got to say, let alone follow me. Hell, even I was fed up with my own life. It was boring, dull and unnoteworthy as far as I was concerned. But to my amazement (and utter bemusement), they did. Why? Because the one thing I did talk about was my longing for change, how stuck I'd been feeling and the lengths I was going to, to make change happen. I shared posts about books I was reading, podcasts I was listening to and how much better they were making me feel. I shared about the different habits I was shaking, and the new ones I was replacing them with, how I'd cut down on eating crap and watching mindless TV and replaced it with learning some new online marketing skills. I shared the reasons I'd decided to start a business online, how I'd planned to quit my career and how much I believed in the business I'd begun. It became a bit of a diary rather than anything else, and although I wasn't actually selling or sharing links on my page, I often invited viewers to message me if they had questions or would like some more information on the business I was building. It worked and really sparked some interest. I still wasn't sharing any videos or lives at this point, but I was sharing the odd photograph of myself and it seemed to be enough.

The reason it worked so well is this. I didn't realise it at the time but everything I was sharing was building my overall credibility and trustworthiness as someone they'd like to learn from. I was open, honest and authentic in my approach to it and came across as very real, relatable and approachable as a result. It wasn't planned, I simply didn't know how to be any other way, but looking back now, it's the exact reason people chose to work with me over anyone else.

You see, you don't have to be some big influencer to attract attention and have an impact, and you don't have to bare your soul either, you just have to get people to know who you are and **remember** you! People are increasingly wary of polished professional types who barely show a glimmer of personality; we're just sick and tired of fakery on social media, aren't we? Show me a mum of three making millions in her pyjamas and I'm all ears.

REVOLUTIONARY TASK

"Your brand is what other people say about you when you're not in the room"

—JEFF BEZOS

In your **#nwmrevolution** workbook, take the time to do a bit of reflection. What do **you want** people to be saying about you while you're not in the room? Does your current social media say that about you? Ask a stranger to give you three words to describe your current brand. Email me your profile link with the title '3 Branding Words' to info@samantha-ayris.com if you're brave enough, and I'll take a look and give you my three-word feedback.

In your **#nwmrevolution** workbook you'll also find more discussion points like the ones below...

- What's your 'BIG WHY'? Why are you building a business, what are you looking to change?
- How can you help others?
- What do you stand for?
- What do you have strong opinions about?

- What three words would you use to describe yourself?
- What three words would your friends use to describe you?

(Going back to the task on values might help you with this)

I know thinking about yourself like this can be difficult and also feel a bit silly, but it's important - because how can you go out there and shine at being you, if you don't truly know who you are, what you stand for and the gifts you have to share with the world? Thinking I was just a nobody with little value to share is something that held me back for at least the first year of my business. This task is going to cut that learning curve completely for you.

If you try marketing to everyone, you'll end up appealing to no one

In the beginning, once they're confident they have an irresistible offer and highly profitable business model under their belt, I always ask my clients to tell me who they'd like to help, and the answer is almost always the same. *'Well, everyone, I'd like to help as many people as possible.'* Sure, we all want world peace and what have you, but the true translation of this phrase is, *'I'll take money from anyone who will buy'*. And that right there is a problem.

Every organisation in the world caters for an 'ideal' customer, client, consumer, whatever you want to call them, because nice as it would be to have everyone and his dog throw their money at us, when you market to everyone you actually appeal to no one. A bit like that old saying *'jack of all trades, master of none'*. I'll explain more about what I mean by that as we go on.

So, before we go on to talk about what to post on social media to build this loyal following, we need to know who we're talking to and who we want to attract. **We do not want to attract everyone and anyone.**

We are all very different individuals and people naturally resonate with people who are more like them, and since you're already a go-getting rockstar, attracting more people just like you will be a piece of cake. You just need to find **your** niche. **Your** people. The ones **you** can connect with and **help**, because you understand how they feel. We call these people your 'avatar'.

The reflection exercise you did earlier in this chapter will probably help you pinpoint the kind of person you're looking to attract, because more often than not, our avatar turns out to be someone very much like us. It's often the person we were before we started out on this journey, because that's the kind of person who needs our help most.

You're well equipped to help and support this person because you know what their problems are, what worries them and what keeps them up at night and most importantly, how you can help solve those problems with what you have to offer.

Even if you're only one small step ahead, you've been there and you're living proof that change is possible.

It drives me crazy how few people actually take the concept seriously. I want to make it clear that this isn't a 'nice to have'; knowing what you're looking for in your perfect team member is 100% essential for success. If you don't know who you're talking to on your social media, what their problems are and how you can help, how will you know what to say to capture their attention? Get your avatar (perfect team member) nailed as a matter of urgency and you'll save yourself a whole lot of head and heartache in the future. Many of those who badmouth our industry are those who should never have been attracted into our teams to begin with, they were probably persuaded, convinced or offered empty promises in order to make a sale, when perhaps they were never quite cut out to be business owners in the first place.

We're not just looking to make sales here, we're looking for highly driven go-getters who are motivated to put in the work and do whatever it takes to transform their lives forever and help thousands of others do the same. And if they're not, but they love your product, for the love of God, just let them buy the product and get on their merry way to enjoy it. No harm done. Stop forcing square pegs into round holes and setting people up to fail. This is exactly where so much of the negativity in our industry emerges from, and we can stop it, here, right now, by nailing our avatar and only ever inviting the right people to build a business with us.

REVOLUTIONARY TASK

This is a biggie, and definitely not one to be missed unless you're prepared for the headaches it will inevitably bring.

In your **#nwmrevolution** workbook (www.nwmrevolution.com/resources) you'll find a comprehensive list of questions for you to answer that will help you get into the head of your avatar. Knowing this information will enable you to:

Create Content that will deeply resonate and have your perfect team member asking for more information.

Connect and Converse with your perfect team member on a level that will have them excited to work with you.

Communicate your offer and magnetically attract members who will slot effortlessly into your team.

Once you've completed this exercise, you'll be so familiar with the type of person you want to attract, that you'll be able to speak directly to their hearts. They'll resonate with your content so deeply that they'll think you got inside their head and are speaking directly to them. Remember the post I told you about that attracted me to this business, the one with the stressed out teacher? That spoke directly to me, my problems and my worries - and look what happened!

CREATING MAGNETIC CONTENT

Without wanting to sound like a stuck record, regardless of where or what you post, what makes your content magnetic is your ability to speak to the needs of, and offer solutions to your avatar's most pressing problems. I'm not going to go into detail here about what you should and shouldn't post, how many times a week, day, hour etc. etc. I'm simply going to say... quality over quantity. Every single post should either educate, inspire or entertain your avatar.

Social media content has one key purpose; relationship building. Not only does it enable you to stand out but positions you as an authority and leader in your niche, which creates immediate credibility. Remember, most people are merely consumers of content, only 1% are actual creators, and simply being one of those puts you head and shoulders above the rest and allows you to stand out in a crowded online space. So don't overthink it!

The purpose of every post you put out there is to take a complete stranger on a journey to becoming a loyal friend and then on into becoming a loyal team member. In order to do that we need to meet them where they're at then show them we understand and support them in finding a way to get them to the place they want to be. Helping them bridge that gap builds trust and sets you up as the perfect person to support them on their future journey.

Creating content can be a huge time suck if you let it, and that's a slippery slope to burnout and content fatigue. Maintaining consistency is important because you want to remain in your audience's minds eye, but don't go posting for the sake of posting. Every single post should be intentional and contribute to the bigger picture. I also advise against beating yourself up about keeping up with every platform and latest craze, if you enjoy it, do it, if you don't, don't!

FEEL, KNOW, DO

Before creating any type of content, you should always ask yourself, what's the purpose of this post? What do I want the person reading this to feel, know and do? This'll keep your content relevant and stop you regurgitating for the sake of having something on your feed that day.

How do I want my avatar to **feel**?

What do I want them to **know**?

What do I want them to **do**? (CTA - Call to Action)

I.e. Like, comment, share, click the link, sign up for a webinar, request more info

Just to make myself super clear here, just like knowing your avatar, a personal brand is not optional. Even if you don't take the time to curate a personal brand for yourself, you'll have one anyway. People will make assumptions about you based on what they hear and see, so it's probably better that you curate that yourself with intentional and creative content, than leave it to chance and end up having a completely different personal brand image than the one you had hoped to portray. If you asked a stranger to give you three words to describe your social media profile and they said something very different to what you were hoping, that's probably what's happened here. You haven't been intentional enough about what you've shared.

Just as your 'personal brand' is what people say about you when you're not in the room, your **content** is the bread-crumb clues you leave behind to get them talking. So what do you **want** them to say about you?

Layer One - Your Key Message - What are you known for and what do you help others to achieve? Be clear about what you do and how you can help.

(Me: *I help network marketers to understand that life doesn't have to be a struggle and support them in building a highly profitable business online with enjoyment and ease.*)

Layer Two - What are you known for amongst your closer circle of acquaintances? What are your strongly held opinions and core beliefs? Sharing these captures attention and creates a connection on a more passion-filled, emotive level.

(Me: *I believe that teaching outdated techniques and tactics is harming the Network Marketing Industry and preventing everyday people from achieving the success they deserve. My mission is to clean up the industry's reputation through re-education and start a revolution that means everyone can proudly become their own success story.*)

Layer Three - Who are you as an individual? What do you love to do in your spare time? What are your hobbies etc.

Sharing these things creates a more personal connection, reveals a deeper authenticity and builds trust and rapport.

(Me: *I love being out in the fresh air, my garden and walking in the countryside. I have two teenage step children, I volunteer as a guide dog puppy trainer and enjoy jumping on the back of my partner's motorbike to blow away the cobwebs.*)

When you mix these up and reiterate them on a regular basis using various post types, your audience will soon get a feel for who you are and what you're about, especially if you convey them using stories.

Our brains are hard-wired for stories, we're attracted to them and we remember them. So while everyone else is talking about products and shouting to be heard, tell your story. Why are you here, where have you come from and what have you had to endure to get this far? What's the transformation? Storytelling speaks straight to the emotional and reptilian part of the brain. Work on becoming your own story of change, then change the lives of others one at a time by using your story to motivate and inspire.

In summary, when posting to build your personal brand, consider the following factors.

1. **Build the *Know, Like Trust* Factor** - People generally only work with those they have taken the time to get to **know**, **like** and **trust**, and these three things are built on authenticity, honesty and

empathy. Be sure to demonstrate this as much as possible in your content.

2. **Become known as the 'go-to' authority in your niche** - how is this piece of content reinforcing the fact that I am knowledgeable, reliable and take my position seriously.
3. **Generate Engagement and Conversation** - Encourage your audience to interact with you, and each other. Ask them questions and engage in conversation with them as much as possible. Be approachable and relatable, we're all human - just be you.
4. **Encourage your audience to take action** - Make sure they know how, or what they can do to take the next step and start working with you.

Visit my free Facebook Group

www.facebook.com/groups/nwmrevolution/

where I regularly share hints, tips and ideas on all of the above.

KEY CHAPTER TAKEAWAYS

- YOU are your brand, not the company you're affiliated with.

- If you choose to separate yourself from the crowd with a Personal Brand, you'll find yourself with a loyal tribe who hang on to your every word.
- Knowing your Avatar inside out is the key to easily creating content that speaks directly to their needs and wants.
- People buy from people they know, like and trust.
- Aim to serve not sell. Long term gains over short term wins.
- Confidence comes with competence - there's no such thing as an unconfident person.

11

AUTOMATION AND SYSTEMS

The Freedom Formula

So, you've got yourself fixed up with a highly profitable business model and an offer that your audience find utterly irresistible because it solves all of their most pressing problems and they can see from your social media and personal brand that you're the expert, the go to person in your niche and that you're the one to help them out.

You have potential new team members banging down the door asking for more information on what you do, and suddenly you've found yourself inundated, with too many people to respond to and not enough time to do it in. You've gone from struggling to make sales, to struggling to keep on top of enquiries for further information. Your diary is full of 1-1 calls with potential customers who want to know more, and you genuinely want to help them all, but you can't. You thought you'd be grateful for such a problem, but the truth is, you're spending all your time on your phone, you're tired and you're missing out on time doing what you want to do. This is not what you were expecting.

This is exactly what happened to me. I felt like I was missing out on sales because I just couldn't keep up, I was exhausted and strangely annoyed at the number of people asking me questions and the amount of time I was having to spend on tedious conversation. I know, there's no pleasing some people.

Like me, many Network Marketers go to great lengths to build a social media presence and a strong following online, but the second they get a bit of interest, it's back to 1-1 calls and endless conversation in the DMs. They pour their time into responding to messages without knowing just how serious they are or whether it's worth their time. (Let's be honest, however tight we are with our avatar, there will always be the odd timewaster looking for something for nothing) While I was a bit miffed about having to spend my time talking to so many random people, others see it as a challenge and the sales vulture vibe kicks back in, it's not a good look!

In this chapter I want to explain to you why I've included 'Automation & Systems' as a vital piece of the Freedom Framework. Pivotal in fact. I'm going to show you how I've automated my entire process to the point where the only people I now speak with are super red hot leads who have already proven their interest with a small investment, have completed several hours of training and either still have questions, or are ready to get started on their business. Not because I don't wish to be helpful, but because I value my time and, well, why do it yourself when an automated system could do just as good a job and also free up more of your time to spend as you please.

But before I go on, I want to address this phrase...

"Oh, but I'm not a techy person"

Suck it up buttercup, neither was I. How much do you want this? Nobody walks into a job knowing what they're doing, we have to learn. Harsh as that may sound, I've heard this phrase so many times before I see it for exactly what it is. Fear. As soon as I start talking about this stuff people always throw in a ton of blocks and barriers my way; reasons why they should just stick to what they know. But as I mentioned in Chapter Ten, confidence comes with competence, and you won't ever become competent at 'the techy stuff' unless you at least give it a try. Remember that toddler who decided to sack off walking and crawl through life? No. It didn't happen. I taught myself how to build a funnel by watching a few videos, and I assure you I'm no tech wizard, yet these days here I am, either teaching others or doing it for them. Overcoming those initial fears and giving this automation malarkey a go is like learning to mine for diamonds. It really isn't rocket science & the return on time and effort invested up-front is mind-blowingly worth it.

A Network Marketing friend of mine told me for years that she '*wasn't a techy person*', until one day I told her enough was enough and listed off all the 'techy' things she'd done, including building funnels for her entire downline. She'd become so used to saying the words that she failed to see that, over time it had become completely untrue. Sometimes you need to call yourself out on your own BS, and if you don't, I will. Go on, give yourself a reality check right now. If you want to see success in your business, you have to be prepared to do things differently and learn some new skills. *If you keep doing what you've always done, you'll always get what you always got*, remember?

So, let's get back to it. Automation is a series of technologies that you can set up to take complete strangers on a journey from being 'intrigued' to an 'excited, brand spanking new team member' all without you needing to be involved in the process. (Worth the effort huh?) Of course, for any business to be successful, what we need is a constant and consistent flow of leads, and people to share our products and opportunities with, and automation is only as good as the leads you feed it with, which is why I bang on so much about knowing how to attract your perfect avatar. Preferably, these leads would also be pre-qualified, and by that I mean, already have a keen interest in what we have to offer and a good understanding of what you do. If you've followed my guidance in the 'Personal Branding' chapter, they most certainly will be. We've also talked alot about attracting potential new team members, rather than chasing them, and what better way to do that than with an aptly named 'Lead Magnet'.

A Lead Magnet

Although in some cases, your social media content may well be enough to attract attention, it stands to reason that you should upgrade to something even more irresistible if you want to grow faster. A lead magnet pretty much does what it says on the tin; it 'magnetises' leads (your perfect team members). I like to think of it as one of those giant magnets that pick up crushed cars, or those red and blue magnets you used to get at school that could pick up a hundred paperclips at a time.

Essentially, a lead magnet is a free, but valuable piece of content such as a PDF, a checklist, a template, a 'How To' guide or similar, uniquely created by you, that offers information suited to your 'perfect team member'. Since you now know your avatar so well, you'll know exactly the kind of information they're looking for as a solution to their most pressing problems, and you can create this just for them. This clever piece of content is offered for free in exchange for their email address. If the customer views the resource as desirable, which they will because you designed it that way, he or she may be willing to exchange their email address for it, so that you can continue sharing information and building the relationship in their inbox. Win-Win. It's a fair exchange whereby the customer can expect to receive emails from you in return for the valuable information you have provided. We'll discuss the purpose of the emails a little further on in the chapter.

The lead magnet itself doesn't have to be anything too profound, but the title needs to be super catchy and something you know with certainty that your avatar will want, need and love. (Solving a problem with your freebie would be even better) Remember though, it also needs to be of high enough quality to reaffirm the fact that you're highly knowledgeable on the subject and the kind of person they'd like to learn more from.

Think of it as dangling a carrot in front of a donkey so you can capture it. I say carrot, because donkeys love carrots (apparently - I'm no donkey expert). That's how the avatar works you see. If I was trying to capture a lion, the carrot wouldn't be my bait of choice; I'd probably use a steak (on a very long pole, while wearing a chainmail suit). Your bait must be irresistible to the exact type of person you're trying to attract. It takes careful thought. Think about the type of thing that you'd have exchanged your email address for before you first started out.

The Funnel

The moment the donkey takes the carrot, is the moment your automation begins (I'm starting to think I should have used a different analogy here, I'm sure your ideal team members are not donkey-like at all; stay with me here). As your ideal customer enters their email address and receives your lead magnet (also known as a freebie), instead of entering into conversation with you, they enter your 'Funnel'.

You may or may not have heard of one of these before, but if this is the first time you've ever come across one, you can thank me later. The sales funnel is **'the'** reason I get to do what I do. The reason I no longer have to get up in a morning and go to work, the reason I get to stay home with my family, the reason I get time to volunteer and play with Guide Dog puppies all day. It's also the reason so many of the people I work with get to travel the world full time or sip champagne in their pyjamas. It buys us back our time. I love it! We live by it! The funnel - what a superb invention!

Funnel = Freedom

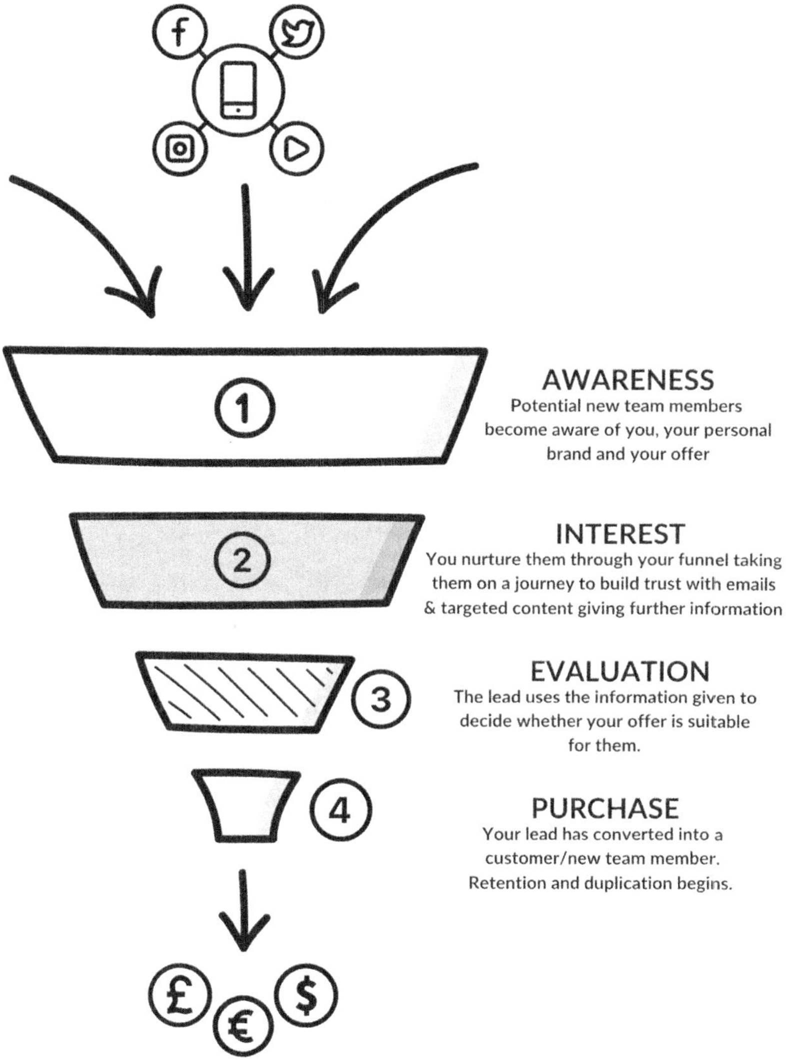

It might look complicated, but a sales funnel is simply a series of pages and stages that are crafted to guide each visitor to the exact action you want them to take. Whether that's signing up for your email list or buying a product - or both.

Without me even having to be present, the funnel takes an intrigued stranger and nurtures them all the way through my sales process. It uses both videos and web based sales pages to teach them what I do and how I can help them, passing on information, answering questions and adding value. Just as you would do in person. Since I know my avatar so well, I already have a good idea what they're looking for, any misconceptions they may have, and of any objections that might come up, so I've set up my trainings and pages to address those and include more evidence by way of testimonials and feedback from other clients as to why working with me or purchasing my offers would be really helpful to them.

So as you can see from the diagram, when someone signs up to receive my lead magnet, via whatever means that may be (any of the social media platforms), the leads get dropped into the top of the funnel. Remember, I don't let just anyone into my funnel, only my ideal team members, because at every step in the process I'm going to be speaking directly to them, to their pains and their pressures and my funnel pages take them on an informative journey towards their ultimate solution. Clever huh?

The Landing Page

The first place your fresh new lead will be sent, before even receiving your lead magnet, will be what's called a 'Landing

Page'. This is a specific page designed to capture the name and email address of the 'lead' before they're sent the information. But it's also so much more than that. The landing page also contains even more information about you, what you do, the kind of people you help etc. You might also leave short testimonials on there from people you've helped in the past with some of your paid products. You don't want anything too over the top here, you're simply setting the scene. Right now, your top priority is guiding them to enter their name and email address, and therefore, your world. You can blow their minds with all the other fabulous stuff later.

Simple as it might seem, there's a great deal of expertise and sales psychology that goes into building these landing pages, even though we're technically just giving something away for free. It's taken a whole load of different designs and a whole lot of testing to get to a point where a high percentage of people who visit the landing pages we've built actually enter their details. You'd be amazed at the number who get as far as clicking to receive the freebie, then back off at the last minute. Online scams have got us suspicious like that, and people are more and more cautious about sharing their details these days, so be sure to stay humble, non-salesy and 100% real here. That kind of behaviour online stands out, I know because I'm told so most weeks.

The Thank you Page (or Tripwire)

The thank you page does exactly that, thanks the lead for their email address and lets them know their freebie is on its way.

But this page can also be used for something else, something super exciting that many people fail to utilise. A 'Tripwire'.

I really don't like this word as it conjures up images of a poor little rabbit getting snared in a trap or something, and as I hope you've already realised, tripping and trapping future team members is totally unnecessary and not the start to the blossoming business relationship I'm looking for. Remember, I'm here to dispel anything remotely shady. A tripwire (although sinister sounding) is actually another attractive, but this time low-priced offer that's designed to turn your lead into a buying customer. The offer should complement the free information they've already requested, but offer a slight step up in value, which makes it worth paying a small fee for. They're usually priced at between £5.00 – £25.00, but I've personally seen more success from the lower end.

It's almost a bit of a, 'while you're here, how do you fancy this?' like when the lady at the check out zaps your items and says, 'And can I interest you in a six pack of Curly Wurleys today?' Sales funnels that nurture you into making purchases exist offline too, you've just probably never realised. They're smart like that.

According to sales psychology, once people have bought an inexpensive item from you, they're more likely to purchase something else. That's the real value of a tripwire. They've dipped their toe in the water, experienced a little bit of what it's like to learn from you and, if you did a great job, are left wanting more. Using this method gives you the best opportunity to support your new buyer even more, once they're in your sales funnel.

The customer, of course, can kindly decline the offer if they so wish, (no thanks to the Curly Wurleys) but would still receive the original freebie.

As you can see, as your potential new team member moves through the funnel, they're nurtured and gently offered more information and opportunities as they go. This all contributes to the *Know, Like and Trust* factor and helps them on their journey from a complete stranger to dedicated follower and friend. Every step they take is a little closer to becoming a valued member of your team, and as of yet, you haven't even had a physical part of that. Where were you? Sleeping? Shopping? Dancing?

At this point, rather than simply directing them back to their emails to collect the freebie, I've had great success in directing them into a private Facebook™ group where I've been able to offer them more information and an opportunity to really get to know me and what I do through videos etc. all for free. A person can be in my world for either a matter of days or years before they're ready to work with me, but once they enter my funnel, they enter my world and unless they choose to unsubscribe, they'll find all manner of things that might be of interest to them, some free, some payable. But what makes them stick around is my laid-back approach to it all, my honest, genuine, straight-talking personal brand and the fact that I've tailored everything around them, the avatar I created on day one. A Facebook™ group is a great place to create a sense of community, support and belonging and is a hugely valuable resource when growing and nurturing an audience. (You can join us here www.facebook.com/groups/nwmrevolution)

The Email Nurture Sequence

The problem with social media profiles and Facebook™ Groups and the like, is that they're not officially our property. I know of people who have lost literally thousands of loyal followers overnight as a result of a social media giant randomly shutting down their account. These things **do** happen, and they happen more than I'd care to admit. Sometimes there's a valid reason, but not always, and trying to get to the bottom of it and recover your losses can be a mission in itself. The solution? An email list.

An email list is a special list of names and email addresses of people who gave you permission to send them updates and promotions from your business. Regardless of what happens, your email list will remain your property, and nobody can take that away from you. (*There are rules to follow with regard to*

GDPR though, so please get yourself familiar with those first) Since they joined your email list by opting in to receive information via your landing page, we know they're already interested in what you have to offer. This is why they're more likely to convert into paying customers further down the line. In many cases, I've actually noticed much higher conversions from my email list than social media, and here's why I believe that to be so.

Firstly, email can be much more personal. It's delivered straight into someone's actual inbox where you can address them directly, by name. In a world full of offers and noise, personal connection counts. Being automated doesn't mean you can't also personalise. I write all my emails as if I'm writing to a friend, because I am!

I know my avatar so well that I know what they're looking for from me and can tailor my emails to suit, and so can you.

From the point that they opt in, I recommend setting up a series of at least five, automated emails. One a day, for five days, just long enough for your lead to get used to you hanging about in their inbox, and then after that, one per week (you don't want to get clingy and annoying).

This first set of emails is called your nurture sequence, also known as a welcome sequence, or onboarding sequence. Whatever you want to call it, it's a series of emails that allow people to get to **know** you, **like** you and **trust** you. Are you starting to see a pattern here? That's right, **everything** we do is about building and nurturing a relationship, and here's why.

Not everyone will be ready to buy from you straight away, not everyone will be ready to work with you and that's ok, the purpose of regular emails is to keep in touch and keep you at the forefront of their minds. You know the saying, out of sight, out of mind. I like to think of it as popping up here and there with a *'yoo hoo, remember me? Here I am being witty and helpful again, would you like a little snack? Snippet? Titbit? No? Ok, see you next week.'* I've had people start working with me years after they first signed up for my freebie, and I didn't even realise they were still around.

Some people (like me) like to snoop around for a while first and get a feel for everything, and when you send them a regular email, it helps them get to know you a little better. They want to know what you had for breakfast and how many times you get up in the night to pee. Just tell them, there really are no rules. Give them what they want. They're curious and they're hungry for more because they want to believe that you're the answer to their problems, and if they're going to spend time or money with you, they need to know it'll be worth it and that you're not going to do a runner on them at the first opportunity. Trust is everything.

Emails are the perfect place for that because it's the place you can just be you, chat like a human and talk about the stuff humans talk about. The emails I open (no I don't open them all, my inbox is a place that would give most people nightmares) are the chatty, helpful ones that don't constantly try to sell to me, from the people who tell me funny stories about their day with a little, "p.s. Have you seen this amazing thing I'm doing, selling etc" at the bottom.

Of course, you can share your offers in your email, but just as we talked about in the Personal Branding chapter, make the content of your emails light, fun, valuable and helpful. Repurposing some of your social media content is absolutely recommended, I'm all for saving time. Just remember, you're not talking to a whole audience anymore. There's a person at the end of that email. Make them feel like it was written just for them.

The Webinar/Masterclass

Something I've found super successful is using a Webinar or Masterclass both as a lead magnet and as something to promote in my emails. You could do the same for your own business. Film up a short presentation video on what you do and how you can help. If it's appropriate you can talk about your products, the benefits, the business and the compensation plan, share your successes, and some social proof and then finish off with a special offer and an opportunity to join you right then and there at the end. Remember to follow my guidance about not coming across as cheesy or salesy. Keep it cool, casual, chatty, raw and real.

I've seen great success with this method, and all it takes is to record your video training once, then pop it into your funnel to be watched over and over again. It goes a little like this.

1. Share information on your forthcoming Masterclass on socials, explain what you'll be teaching and how you can help your avatar (make them feel like you're speaking directly to them, you've been in their shoes and can help, remember!?). Make it appealing by being solution focused and bespoke to your avatar's needs and wants. Use some of the content ideas I shared earlier or in my private community www.facebook.com/groups/nwmrevolution if you're stuck.
2. Share your 'landing page' domain with those who show interest so they can become 'leads' by entering their name and email address to access your funnel process.
3. Your lead enters their details and is sent straight to the Webinar (which you've set up in your funnel) to watch and learn more.
4. Either they sign up to work with you at the end of the webinar; Or
5. You follow up with them via automated email to see what they thought, answer any questions, clear up any misconceptions and close the sale.

Bingo! Easy as that! The only thing you physically had to do (if anything) was answer the odd question via email at the end.

Having said that, more often than not, if you make your

webinar simple and clear enough, most will go ahead and sign up using the automated payment page at the end of the webinar. Bish, bash, bosh. Done. Money appears in your account a few days later, and everybody's happy!

Now that's automation! Tell me again why you're not doing this already?

REVOLUTIONARY TASK

In your **#nwmrevolution** workbook

(www.nwmrevolution.com/resources) I want you to brainstorm some 'Lead Magnet' ideas. Thinking about your ideal team member and the problems they currently face on a day-to-day basis, what do you think might help them? What do they ask Google for help with? What's the one thing that keeps them up at night, that you have a solution for?

Once you have a few ideas, do a little research and see if you can find anything similar out there. You'll also find some ideas at www.nwmrevolution.com/resources

12

LEVERAGING SOCIAL MEDIA

The Rocket fuel

Once you're fully automated, your only limitation is how many new members you can cope with adding into your team and educating each week, but even then, this can be fully automated too. Although I personally support all my clients when they need it, my entire training and educational platform is fully automated. I've pre-recorded videos that train members on every step of the process, address misconceptions and encourage focus, discipline and continued action, as well as hold their hand and demonstrate some of the tricker bits. This allows new business owners to work at their own pace. It's a team leader's duty to teach their members to become as independent as possible, as soon as possible, and an automated system allows for that perfectly. It's counterproductive for them to cling onto your apron strings for too long.

Leveraging Social Media

This all sounds great, but so far, we've been relying heavily on our social media presence to attract leads organically (for free) into our business. Not having to pay a penny for your leads is a huge benefit in itself, and massively improves your profit margin, but...

What I promised you at the beginning of this book was time freedom and a business you could build with enjoyment and ease. I strongly maintain that having a solid personal brand is the backbone of your business and that consistent content will act as supporting evidence to confirm that you are exactly who you say you are and are of course an authority in your niche and 'the' person to work with. But when you're also relying on this content to bring in a consistent flow of leads who are genuinely interested in working with you, the pressure is on to be ever-present, everywhere. Step away for a moment and that steady flow of leads could soon start to slow. It can be challenging to keep on top of all the platforms, the newest trends, algorithm changes etc. etc. and there's so much chatter that it's hard to know who to listen to, and each time a new idea is released the learning curve starts all over again.

But what if the purpose of your content was to merely *maintain* visibility and support your personal brand, and your leads came in automatically from elsewhere? Would that **ease** the pressure? Would that make creating content **enjoyable** again?

In this instance, what you could do is 'buy' that time back by paying for your posts to appear under the noses of the very people you want to see them. I'm talking about paid social media advertising. For whatever reason, some people find this prospect utterly terrifying, but over the course of this chapter I hope to prove to you why leveraging paid advertising to scale your business is not only exciting, but potentially highly, highly (yes two highlys) profitable and a complete no brainer.

Before I go any further, I'd like to spend a moment reminding you that however small you may feel right now, if you have a Network Marketing business, **you are** a professional business owner and this chapter **is** for you. For some reason, (probably one of the many reasons covered in previous chapters actually, other people's opinions, lack of confidence, miseducation etc.) network marketers have a tendency to limit themselves, keep themselves small and make every move with a 'this is just a side hustle' mentality. But it really doesn't have to be. Remember, when you treat it like a profession, it'll pay you like a profession, and professionals invest in their businesses to help them grow.

I think the reason many people shy away from paid ads is because it requires you to invest money upfront with no immediate return. Well that, my friends, is what business owners do, they take risks.

In the words of Mark Zuckerberg, **"the biggest risk is not taking any risks"**. By not investing in levelling up your business and implementing all the new and exciting things I've taught you throughout this book, you're risking staying in the very same place you're in right now, and still complaining about the same old things two, five or even ten years from now. How does that sound?

So, back to the ads... We've all seen adverts in our social media feeds. Those posts that are labelled as 'sponsored' means that someone has paid Meta™ (or whichever platform you're scrolling through) to put that post on your feed.

And that's what we do...

All you have to do is create an advert or post to explain what you have to offer. Now, just as a little caveat, we're not directly selling products here because most platforms have rules that disallow this, but what you can do is promote your 'Lead Magnet' freebie or webinar and send people directly to your landing page where the automation will lead them through the rest of the process.

The most exciting part about social media advertising is that platforms hold so much detailed data about its users, you and I included. Do you ever find that ads pop up in your feed about things you've been thinking about? It's creepy isn't it? Big Brother really is watching you, and every time you click, hover, watch or read something, that information is stored and added to your own personal digital footprint. How do you think all this Artificial Intelligence is created? From the data they're collecting about us, every second of every day. What's amazing is that this data is ethically available to business owners and advertisers like us to benefit from. One of the main reasons social media marketing is so effective is that brands can hyper-target individuals based on their exact demographics and interests.

And here's where the importance of our avatar comes in again. If your avatar is a female between 25-35, loves health and fitness, designer handbags and lives in the UK, you can have your advertisement placed on the feeds of every female in the UK that fits that description.

You can choose any age, gender, demographic, job title, interest or hobby, you can target people with specific shopping habits, parents of teenagers, people from specific income brackets, and from anywhere in the world. You can even target people who are interested in a particular brand, your Network Marketing company even.

We're not just talking about advertising to the masses hoping someone might buy, we can be uber-specific, and when you only put your offer in front of the people who you know are already interested - the chances of someone taking you up on your offer are inevitable.

Thousands of interested potential team members can be viewing and clicking on your sponsored post, Every. Single. Day.

You can sponsor posts for as little as £1 per day (though I do recommend spending a bit more than that as it's 100% worth it) and have your automated funnel flooding with new and exciting leads to nurture in your inbox, follow you on social media, watch your webinars, join your groups, buy your stuff and become superstar team members.

And for those of you still worried about spending up front, the typical return on ad spend (ROAS) is between 5x and 30x, depending on your offer. That means for every £1 we spend on ads, we get between £5 -£30 back in sales. Spend £500 and get £2500 - £15,000 (approx $18,000) back.

Suddenly, spending hours cold messaging hundreds of random leads a day seems silly, doesn't it? That's because when you compare it to how professional network marketers work, it is.

Although many, many network marketers achieve their own version of success with organic (free) content, you can see how spending on Social Media Advertising is like pouring rocket fuel on the fire. And that's why you need an automated system set up, to help you keep on top of the many leads that will inevitably start rolling in on auto pilot.

Yet even after having seen these figures and the huge return on investment, many network marketers remain afraid to spend their hard earned cash on building their business. All other businesses require investment, why would network marketing be any different? I get it, shifting from employee mindset and into professional business owner can be tough and the fear based stories we tell ourselves like 'money doesn't grow on trees' come flooding back to us. I spent a lifetime believing that money was hard to come by and that rich people were all arrogant arses (remember those suits with frowns and the mean parents in Chapter One). Then I started making a bit of money and got to know a few of those 'rich arses'. They're actually some of the nicest people I know. I recognised quite early on that if I was going to make a go of this, I had to go all in, so I borrowed £7,000 to invest into my business to give me a leg up. What's that saying? You've got to speculate to accumulate? Just the thought of owing that kind of money made me want to vomit, (yet I was completely fine with the idea of owing thousands for a car that was no longer worth what I owed, funny that) but as it turns out it was the best £7,000 I've ever spent. It allowed my business to grow, flourish and thrive. Who knows where I'd be today if I hadn't taken that terrifying leap. Now I continue to invest in my business every single day, because I know that every penny I spend will come back to me 5x, 10x, 30x and more.

According to Jonathan Durante, Forbes magazine; there's no doubt that the business world is changing rapidly, and it's up to each business to stay on top of current marketing trends or get left behind. Brands will need to find new ways to market and sell and will have to adapt to the current times to do so. Those who are not leveraging digital marketing may be missing out on key strategies that can increase performance and results even more.

Don't let that be you. Embrace the challenge, embrace the change, and run with it. I'll ask you again. How badly do you want to achieve those goals and that monthly income to enable it to happen? Are you willing to do what it takes to get there? Even if it means investing up front? You have access to a hugely lucrative industry right there in the palm of your hands, it's your duty to do everything possible to make it work for you, your family and the many, many team members whose lives you're going to change as a result.

Having a Network Marketing Business and not using ads and automation is like owning a pair of brand new Louboutins and a Lamborghini, then leaving the shoes in the box and the car in the garage.

A crime. A terrible, terrible waste.

KEY CHAPTER TAKEAWAYS

- Ease the pressure and make creating content enjoyable again by using it to merely maintain visibility. Let the ads bring in your flurry of targeted leads.
- In the words of Mark Zuckerberg, **"the biggest risk is not taking any risks"**.

- Ethically make use of the 'Big Brother' data that social media platforms collect on us, to specifically target your exact avatar.
- The typical return on ad spend (ROAS) is between 5x and 30x depending on your offer.
- Don't let the fear of putting the money in upfront prevent you reaping the rewards on the other side.

13

COMMUNITY AND MENTORSHIP

The Backup

"A mentor is someone who sees more talent and ability within you, than you see in yourself, and helps bring it out of you."

— BOB PROCTOR

If this is all new to you, I suspect that you might be feeling a little overwhelmed by now, like you might have bitten off a little more than you can chew and that you're struggling to know where to even start. Or maybe you're feeling so fired up that you just want to get cracking right away. Yes, it can feel a little daunting in the beginning, but I **know** this is possible for you, and all it's going to take now is a little courage to step away from the all too familiar failures and towards those amazingly audacious goals you set yourself. Terrified at the prospect? Understandable, but there's really no need to be, because I've got your back. My team, and everyone I work with in this incredible industry, we all have your back, because every single one of us are excited to see you thrive in a way that so many other network marketers fail to see.

Outside of network marketing, online coaching and mentorship can involve the kind of money that has you remortgaging your house. Sure, there are coaches out there who are worth every penny and more, and many people would kill to work with them (I have a few in mind right now), but in our industry, mentorship is available to us for free, because it's in our uplines interest for you to do well. That in itself is a huge plus point. Unfortunately (or fortunately, whatever the case may be) the quality of your upline, mentor, leader, whatever you want to call them, is down to the luck of the draw. Regardless of your opinion, 99% of the time they probably mean well, but it's important to remember that they're on their own journey too, and can sometimes miss the mark and fail to meet your expectations. Sometimes that's a case of misguided expectation (your success is not their responsibility and they're not there to do the work for you, if it's not working it's down to you to change that, not them) and sometimes, they're just not ready to lead yet. I've definitely experienced both of these and hold my hands up and admit, I was winging it for quite some time before I became anywhere near inspirational. Be grateful for the person that introduced you to your business, but don't hinge your success on their actions (or inactions) as a leader.

The beauty of being part of a systems driven opportunity rather than the typical upline dependent MLM is that you don't need to be reliant on anyone. The only human variable is you, the rest is down to the already proven, duplicatable technology that gives you all you need to succeed at your own pace. It's up to you what you do with it, based on your goals and circumstances. Having a knowledgeable upline or mentor to support you in that is just an added bonus, not a necessity.

Your business is your business. When I started out, my direct upline spoke to me a grand total of around three times in DMs before disappearing off the face of the planet. I have a lot to be grateful for, because that meant I had to go out there and find my own way. There were plenty of other leaders out there offering their support, don't get me wrong, and I'm super grateful for that, but I believe a lot of my success has been down to my own tenacity and a determination to make things work no matter what. As a result I've become quite the 'no nonsense' leader when it comes to team members expecting to be spoon fed. Whilst it's important to have your own cheerleader, it's also important to know that this person will also be your critic when required. Just like how my friends can depend on me to tell them when they're being a lovesick doormat, anyone who works with me knows that if I think they're in need of a kick up the arse, I'm not afraid to give it. As I said way back in Chapter Three, sometimes you need someone to tell you what you *need* to hear, not what you *want* to hear, and if that's the difference between success and failure, bring it on.

I asked some of the ladies I've supported recently for their thoughts on mentorship. This is what they said...

"You want someone who can provide you with the tools & guide you but not do it all for you. The only way you learn & grow is by taking action yourself. They are there to support & advise, having started their journey just like you, they understand the obstacles & emotional setbacks you may have. They know how hard it can be, so they are there to champion you at each milestone & lead you onto the next."

— CLAIRE

"Your mentor should have paved the way for you, they hit the hurdles and overcame them. That's important because they will help guide you over any obstacles in your way. Remember, they have felt how you do, they understand the highs and lows as you hit them. They have pushed through and with the right mentor so will you."

— JO

Whilst I agree with their interpretation, I see my role as much simpler than that, and I'll sum it up in one word. EASE. It's my job to shorten the learning curve for each person I work with, to make it as EASY as possible for them to succeed by providing them the tools, the knowledge and the skillset. And that's where so many mentors go wrong. Somehow they manage to make it about them with their need to feel needed. I want my students to feel confident enough to fly the nest as soon as possible. That's when I know I've done a good job. But when the tools and the skillset they're teaching makes everything feel like hard work, there are less highs to celebrate and the ass kickings get personal, because it's not actually you that's doing it wrong, it's the outdated systems and strategies that are not working in your favour. You should never be afraid to separate yourself from the pack if you feel the need to. Just because your upline introduced you to your business, you owe them nothing. If you find a better way that suits you, you should 100% go with it. Your business. Your way. Always.

Mentorship and community go hand in hand, and maybe, like I once did, you're wondering why I've included being part of a community as the final key plate in my Plate Spinning System. Surely it's not essential? If that's how you feel, you probably haven't found a community of 'your' people yet. I've been part of my fair share of cliquey, cheesy, faux friendly groups. Sure everyone means well (I think), but I'm never 100% sure how authentic they are. Are they really living the lives they say they are? Do they really want to befriend and support me, or am I just another £/$ sign in their eyes? It's so hard to tell. You can get a much better impression when you meet people offline can't you, your intuition can tune in much more accurately.

I recently hosted a large offline event for the online network marketing community I'm part of. It wasn't my first rodeo, I've been involved in many such events, and although it comes as no surprise to me these days, the energy in such a room is still unlike any other. It's tangible. Electric! But why? It's weird, and very difficult to explain, or for anyone who hasn't experienced this to understand, but I'll try to put it into words.

Imagine this, you started a network marketing business online and you joined this online community of people in the same boat, some were new just like you, but others had a bit more experience under their belts. You occasionally talk to them on community video calls (or just listen in because actually, talking on those things terrifies you) and chat in DMs to people you personally resonate with. You know each other, but you don't really *'know'* each other. Then someone announces this big offline event and you jump at the chance because, well, FOMO[1] and the hosts have made it sound like it's going to be pretty awesome. You and your 'friends' book a ticket each and you're massively excited to go.

Then the day (or the night before) arrives and you start to feel sick! You suddenly realise that you don't actually know these 'friends' at all, and what was some exciting business event has started to feel like some sort of sordid blind date. What were you thinking? What if he/she's a complete weirdo? I'm going to feel like such a loner. Who do I think I am and how on earth did I get sucked into all this?

You arrive at the venue and head straight for the toilets to hide and pull yourself together. You notice a small window above the toilet, too small to climb out. Damn. (You hear of people doing this on blind dates don't you, I've never done it personally but my friend once escaped through the kitchen of a restaurant leaving the poor guy to eat on his own at the table. Hilarious at the time, but looking back… that poor guy!)

You finally pluck up the courage to walk in, you bump into a few people you recognise and they fling their arms around you. Instantly you feel relieved that they're not weirdos and thankfully, they're actually exactly the same in real life as they are online, only either a lot shorter or taller than you'd thought. (I'm 5ft 1 and somehow that always seems to come as a surprise, maybe I have the head and shoulders of a tall person?? Is that a thing?) Anyway, the conversation starts flowing and you realise that you're actually more at home with these people than your actual friends. You have so much in common, you have shared goals and ambitions and they seem to understand things your 'real life' friends just don't get. The connection is magical, the energy is electric and you finally feel like you've found your people, the people that finally understand you. There isn't an ounce of negativity in the room and that's mind-blowingly refreshing and unlike anything you've ever experienced before.

What I'm describing here is my experience, meeting my tribe, my community, in the early days. I don't know if this is the same for you and where you hang out? If it's not then maybe you haven't yet found yours yet and you should keep looking. The feeling you get from standing in a room full of like-minded people cannot be dismissed. You'll know it when you find it. It's powerful. I sometimes wonder if that's why people call us 'cult-like', because most people have never experienced being in a room of people who genuinely have your back, with zero negativity. And you know what these 'Negative Nellies' say about things that sound too good to be true (it probably is). We must all have been *brainwashed* or something. God forbid! As I said right at the beginning of the book, if you ask me, there are plenty of people out there with stinky attitudes who could do with a good brainwash, a good scrub inside and out. *'Wash your mouth out with soap and water'* as my mum would say. If it means you come out the other side happier, kinder, more fulfilled and living a life you enjoy, I'm all for it; get scrubbing!

The beauty of online communities is that they bring people from all corners of the globe into one place, together. We humans are social beings, we thrive most when we're supporting each other, and can achieve so much more than we can alone. As part of a community we can facilitate change and drive evolution on a much grander scale. When we connect around a shared common purpose, our connection is an opportunity for us to learn, share and collaborate with each other, which in turn can foster growth and further inspiration.

It's another cheesy overused phrase, but we really do 'rise by lifting others'.

Have you ever been asked that question about 'being a good team player' in an interview? I've been asked this so many times in the past; I always lied. To be honest, I always thought I worked better on my own, I never said that of course, but give me a bit of independence and responsibility and you can guarantee I'd run with it. The truth is, I always felt held back by having to collaborate with others at work, but that's not the answer they want to hear is it.

But now, as I sit here in my home office, alone, my answer is very different. Collaboration and bouncing off other people is essential for growth. It sparks creativity and inspiration, and seeing others do well also sparks a bit of healthy competition in you too. These are all things we can't always get from the people in our immediate circle, despite them meaning well.

Sad but true, but the people around you in 'real life' are often not on the same wavelength, the same page or even the same planet on some occasions, and find it difficult to understand what we do. You stepped outside of societal norms and started doing things differently, that makes it difficult for others, who haven't, to comprehend sometimes.

However much we shout about how amazing it is to have the freedom to work from home, working alone online is a quiet, lonely place. Even for a self confessed introvert like me who

loves her own company, if you don't tap into the community available to you, you'll eventually start to spiral.

True to the 'non team player' persona I'd given myself, for a short while I decided I didn't need to be part of some community of internet strangers to be successful, but I was wrong. I soon started to feel isolated, unsupported and out on a limb, lacking inspiration and eventually, motivation and drive.

So ask me again. Am I a good team player? Hell yes, so much so that I've built my own community of network marketing go-getters (and we're starting a Revolution by the way, did you know?). The difference is, unlike in a job where you're matched up with an eclectic bunch of people we call colleagues (and would rarely choose as friends in many cases) I attracted a very particular type of person into my community from day one, my go-getting, focused and highly driven avatar. People who share my vision for a better life, people I will resonate with and vice versa. My tribe. My soon to be friends for life.

We humans were not built to work alone. As a species we evolved in small groups like a wolf pack, so thrive when we're surrounded by others.

But not just anyone.

They've got to be the **right** people, and that's key. Motivational speaker Jim Rohn famously said that '*we are the average of the five people we spend the most time with*', and although you might have heard that bounded around social media a million times before, there really isn't a better way to put it. When it comes to those closest to us, we're greatly influenced, whether positively or not. What *they* say and do affects the way we think, our self-esteem, and our decisions, so choosing them carefully is imperative.

Similarly, your diet is not just what you eat, but what you consume in general, what you watch, what you read and the voices and opinions you listen to, it all has an impact; positive or negative. So that said, be sure you're part of a community that nourishes your mind with only the highest quality vibes. And don't fall for any of that 'toxic positivity' crap either. If it feels off, it probably is. Get out while you can. When you find your people you'll know, it's a bit like when you get that funny feeling inside when you realise you've found *'the one'* and as one of my community members so eloquently put it recently, when you find your people *'it just feels like home'*.

Here are a few more things some of my wonderful community members have said:

"I've held a fair few jobs and always thought I had the support of my colleagues, but since joining this community I've realised that ***this*** *is real genuine support. Everyone is genuinely excited for you, your business, your personal growth, development and your journey.*

No matter your question, query or worry someone will always be there to help and offer advice and guidance; and to think we are all strangers just meeting through a life changing opportunity. I truly feel excited everyday reading people's posts, seeing their stories and watching their videos. I'm forever grateful for finding this community and finally finding somewhere I can relate with so many people and share this wonderful journey with them all."

— **CHARLI**

"I didn't understand the importance of a community until I was part of one. It's a place to express yourself, learn and grow without being judged. Instead you are supported every single step of the way. You have people cheering for you more than you cheer for yourself! Being part of a community like this has really helped me grow individually as a person. I'm so grateful that I'm surrounded by people who accept me for who I am and support me all the way, which leads to me being the best person I could ever be for myself, my family and everyone around me including the people I help daily. My business would not be where it is today if it wasn't for the community that's supported me since day one."

— ***SANDRA***

Since starting my online journey there hasn't been a day where I haven't felt inspired. You get to learn from the more experienced and we all get to grow together. It never feels like there is a hierarchy, just everyone supporting each other, sharing knowledge and wanting the best for you. Being part of a community has definitely kept me going and had a positive impact on me, it's also a huge part of why I enjoy building my business.

— ***NICOLA***

I guess that's where the 'enjoyment' part comes in. It doesn't matter how rough or tough the road, when you're surrounded by your very own troop who spur you on and carry you when you're down, then dance, sing and shout from the rooftops when you're winning - you can't go wrong. They won't let you. Stay connected. Not using the community and connections available to you is like drilling a hole in the bottom of your bucket, the focus, drive and inspiration will slowly drip out and your business will eventually run dry.

KEY CHAPTER TAKEAWAYS

- Stay connected. Without the support of like-minded people you'll start to feel isolated, out on a limb, lacking inspiration and eventually, motivation and drive.
- Avoid toxic positivity like the plague.
- When you find your tribe, you'll know.
- A mentor's job is to make building a business feel easy and enjoyable.
- What you watch, what you read and the voices and opinions you listen to, all have an impact; positive or negative. Drown out the negativity by surrounding yourself with the right kind of noise.
- You are the sum of the five people you spend the most time with. Choose wisely.

REVOLUTIONARY TASK

If what I've spoken about through this book has resonated with you (which I suspect it has if you've got this far) then there are many more like you in my #NWMRevolution Community. You can join us at www.facebook.com/groups/nwmrevolution.

Using the hashtag #nwmrevolution I'd love for you to share on your socials your biggest takeaways from this book, so others can share in that too. What are you going to implement? Are you joining the revolution?

FINAL WORDS

A revolution at its core boils down very simply to individual people, their choices and their actions, and led by a small but mighty pioneer such as myself, with the vision and commitment to see it through, we have tremendous power to begin, grow and sustain positive revolutionary change within our industry. For everyone.

This book is my plea for you to join me. Let's put a stop to the outdated techniques that are tarnishing our reputation and show everyone what a successful, professional network marketing business looks like.

I'm not asking you to go burning your bra or marching the streets with banners. I simply ask that you take the time to improve your own business using the 'Freedom Framework' found in this book, share the book with your team and learn to effortlessly spin one plate at a time. For when others see you succeeding with ease, enjoyment and pride, they'll think twice, and maybe, just maybe, they'll want you to teach them how to spin plates too.

You as an individual have the power to create a ripple effect in our industry by using the 'Freedom Framework' to smash every audacious goal you set yourself during this process and by sharing your success and positive experiences that have authenticity, honesty and integrity at the heart of them.

For support in implementing the Freedom Framework into your own business, or in creating a business from scratch go to www.nwmrevolution.com/call to book a 15 minute chat. Nobody needs to struggle, the tools and the support are right there.

LET'S USE THEM TO START A NETWORK MARKETING REVOLUTION!

"First they asked me why I was doing it.

Now they ask me how they can too!"

— SAMANTHA AYRIS

#NWMREVOLUTION

CASE STUDIES

Hayley's Story - Making up for Lost Time as a Mum

Hayley had worked three jobs for as long as she could remember and felt she'd lost out on so many years with her son. Exhausted and run down, she became completely withdrawn from the outside world and in her own words had 'forgotten who Hayley was'.

Worried she wouldn't know how, Hayley doubted her own ability to use 'The Freedom Framework' to run her business, but pushed past the fear after watching many other 'ordinary' women running their businesses online around their children with relative ease.

Fast forward 2.5 years, Hayley has reduced the number of hours she works per week right down and runs her network marketing business on automation in the background. She recently celebrated a £12k month, is more fulfilled than ever before and can be much more present for her now fourteen year old son. Hayley loves nothing more than helping other unfulfilled mums find their purpose through online business and teaches them the strategies that enabled her to become the success she has.

Adam's Story - From Bored Finance Worker to Full Time Travel

Several years ago Adam's dreams of travelling were slowly slipping away as he worked his socks off in a soul destroying finance office with screaming customers and no hope of a pay rise. After several failed attempts at making some extra money in things like forex trading, dropshipping and matched betting he stumbled across Network Marketing. By using the 'Freedom Framework' Adam was able to target very specific customers and share his offer on automation while he and his wife went out to work. By 2019 he'd made enough to allow both he, and his wife to quit their jobs, sell up and start travelling full time whilst also teaching other travel addicts how they could do the same with a series of pre-filmed videos and trainings. They'd successfully swapped their daily commutes for stress-free beach life and working just a few hours a day, thanks to the automation he'd set up from day one. To date, they've visited 23 countries and recently achieved another of their goals, which was to fly business class across the world!

Harriet's Story - A Lesson in Never Giving Up

Have you ever heard the story of the miner who gave up three feet from gold?

When Harriet joined her Network marketing business she was 25 and working for the British police force, but desperately wanted more. All she wanted was to replace her £1,500 a month salary to go backpacking for a year.

In Harriet's words, that first year was a '*shit show*', making a grand total of £2,145. But knowing that consistency was key, she knuckled down and learnt more about automation and the 'Freedom Framework'. By the end of year two she'd made over £22k, saw her way out and bought a one way ticket to Bali. By this point, Harriet had surrounded herself with a community of super positive, driven people and realised that she'd been holding herself back by playing small, despite the tools and skills she'd now accumulated. Her fear of investing in paid advertising on the front end to produce quality leads and sales out the other end is what had been holding her back. So she went all in.

"And, here I am today, writing this, having just celebrated a £55,000 month. Just a smidge more than my original £1,500 goal. I never believed network marketing could become so

passive and sustainable, but it truly has changed my life and I will never go back.

I now get to invest my profits into other projects that will provide further passive income for a lifetime.

Although it took me a few years to get here, I can see why it's so important to consider the long-term vision. Imagine if I'd have quit after my £2,145 year. It doesn't bear thinking about. A few years is nothing in the grand scheme of things"

WORK WITH SAMANTHA

The teachings shared here within this book are just the tip of the iceberg when compared with the trainings available in Samantha's Marketing Academy. If you'd like to learn more about the different ways you can leverage the Freedom Framework and work with Samantha, whether you have an existing business or not, visit www.nwmrevolution.com/call

You can also join the FREE Network Marketing Revolution Community here www.facebook.com/groups/nwmrevolution

ABOUT THE AUTHOR

Samantha Ayris is a Motivational Speaker, Internationally Accredited Coach and High-Ticket Network Marketing Strategist.

Having worked hard all her life, yet still never quite having much to show for it, at 40 years old Samantha decided enough was enough. She quit a professional teaching career and built her own six-figure online network marketing business from scratch, with zero experience.

A self confessed introvert, her journey has not been without its challenges and experiencing a complete overhaul of every aspect of her life means she's now well equipped to support anyone in transforming from feeling 'stuck in a rut to kicking life's butt'. Her signature system, 'The Freedom Framework' teaches everyday people how to live extraordinary lives by using professional strategies many assume are reserved for the likes of huge corporations and those with huge budgets. Samantha teaches these concepts in a way that even the most technically challenged can understand, and opens doors for the everyday person to take advantage of the highly sought after time freedom and financial rewards it brings.

Samantha takes pride in leading 'The Network Marketing Revolution' #nwmrevolution and in writing this book has set her sights on cleaning up the reputation of the industry once and for all and demonstrating that, with the right strategy and a little tenacity, success, whatever that looks like for you, is inevitable.

You can join Samantha's Network Marketing Revolution Community here.

www.facebook.com/groups/nwmrevolution

Further information can be found at

www.nwmrevolution.com

Follow Samantha Here:

facebook.com/samantha.ayris.94

instagram.com/samantha_ayris

BOOK SAMANTHA AS A SPEAKER

A witty host, compere and speaker with 15 years stage experience in the entertainment industry, Samantha brings energy and excitement as well as a truck-load of motivation, 'hell yeah' moments and a good dose of no nonsense real talk.

You can find further information and view her speaker showreel here www.nwmrevolution.com/speaker

Samantha can be booked as an MC and compere for events, or for an individual speaking slot. She is happy to speak about any of the topics in this book plus...

The Lion Inside - Finding the courage and confidence to be a leader, not a follower.

(Not so) Loud and Proud - Louder doesn't always mean more confident. The Introverts Guide to being silent but deadly.

Finding the Breakthrough

For Network Marketers and Online Business Owners.

It starts with YOU - Authority, Authenticity and Integrity in Social Media

SPEAKER TESTIMONIALS

Sam closed out a recent event with a dynamic talk about finding your inner ROAR! She bounced onto the stage and held the audience captive from the start. Her energy, passion and desire came across in bucket loads and she had everyone on their feet in no time! Sam is a motivational speaker who engages with her audience in a way that only a true professional can. I would have no hesitation in recommending her to speak at any corporate conference, networking event or educational programme - if you are looking to inspire and motivate your team to feel more confident and slay dragons, then get Sam on speed dial now.

— FIONA BRYAN, MANAGING DIRECTOR, DEVELOPING LEADERS LTD

From the moment she started speaking, to the moment she stepped off that stage, she had every single person in the room hooked to every word she was saying.

Sam is one of the most incredible and engaging speakers I've ever had the privilege of listening to.

— PRASHANSHA SHARMA,
FLYING SOLO

BOOK SAMANTHA AS COMPERE

I've been to 4 incredible events now where Sam has been the host and compere.

And WOW! Sam is masterful in the art of building suspense and excitement. She always manages to get the whole room engaged from the outset, raise the roof and have everyone on their feet. Every piece of music and every moment is carefully and skilfully curated.

I've also watched her interact with high profile speakers such as Entrepreneur Rob Moore and Eddie Hall, unplanned yet with ease and confidence. If you want high vibration and an energetic stage presence then Sam should always be the first choice.

— KIRSTY L. RAVEN - CHAMPIONS 4 CHANGE

"Where Sam goes, energy flows". Literally! Every time I've seen Sam take the stage as MC, everyone in the room is on the edge of their seats, because we simply know she's got something spectacular in store for us. And spectacular, you might wonder? Let me explain! It's like an explosion of energy, excitement, dancing, movement. Yes, there's simply no way to stay put when Sam grabs the microphone. Now whilst she's doing an incredible job in building up the energy in the room, let's not forget about the fact that with a wise choice of motivational words and actions throughout, she manages to keep the audience focused for the entire day. What else could you ask for?

— LIANNE VROEGH - FOUNDER OF UNFOLD YOUR FREEDOM

MUSINGS

2. ESCAPING THE SHADY DRUGS RING

1. *My super short hair was a choice, not as a result of some culty ritual - if you've seen my school photos, the ones with perm 3x the size of my head, you'll understand why.*

3. TOUGH LOVE

1. *OG = Original Gangsters - not 'actual' gangsters, as exciting as that might be, just the top network marketers of the time*

10. PERSONAL BRANDING AND AN ATTENTIVE AUDIENCE

1. Which is, ironically what you're likely to get by suggesting to a hormonal forty something that she might want to lose weight, one too many times

13. COMMUNITY AND MENTORSHIP

1. Fear Of Missing Out

Printed in Great Britain
by Amazon

47223432R00119